EASTER
A Pictorial Pilgrimage

EASTER
A Pictorial Pilgrimage

Pierre Benoit, O.P., *Senior Editor*

Pastor Konrad Leube, *Associate Editor*

Elhanan Hagolani, Ph.D., *Editorial Director*

ABINGDON PRESS
Nashville - New York

EASTER
A Pictorial Pilgrimage

Michael Lutin, David Jobling, *Translators*

Marvin Grosswirth, *Executive Editor*   Joseph Jarkon, *Production*

Carol S. Sanders, *Assistant Editor*   Amos Kazimirski, *Graphics and Design*

Werner Braun, *Photography*

Standard Book Number 687-11495-0

Manufactured in the U.S.A. by Unibook, Inc., 215 Park Avenue South, New York, N. Y.

FOREWORD

The New Testament is read by the peoples of the world not as a treatise of history—its historical "data" being somewhat equivocal—but because of an interest in the way and the life of Jesus Christ. Such study contributes significantly to one's own realization of Jesus' objectives: His love for His fellow man and His readiness to bear the cross for the sake of that love.

Throughout the Christian era, pilgrims have flocked to the Holy Land in an effort to personally experience, as closely as possible, the deeds and the sufferings of Christ, hoping, by actually visiting the places He visited, to achieve a closer affinity with Him. Most of these places have recently been proven to be legendary; nevertheless, they still have great historical value for the visitors since they have been venerated by many pilgrims throughout the centuries. Among these many pilgrims was a Galilean nun, Egeria, who travelled through the Holy Land at the end of the fourth century and was the first to report extensively of her travels. Her account was followed by many others, reaching their peak in abundance during the Crusades (eleventh and twelfth centuries).

These reports reveal an interesting fact: despite their having been written at various periods in history, the religious experience remains constant, so that even today, the pilgrim can move closer to Jesus by visiting these same cities, many of which remain unchanged. This brings us to the purpose of this book.

The present work is not an attempt to present still another report of a pilgrimage. It is, rather, an attempt to take the reader on his own pilgrimage, to help him relive, by viewing the Holy Places and seeing the works of art wrought with devotion, the life and the passion of Jesus. It is our hope that these pictures will reveal the charm of a landscape, the ambience of a room, the emotion of an event. We have tried to capture something of the spirit that imbued the people who built these places and adorned them.

Readers who have visited Jerusalem personally will find their memories rekindled by many of the photographs, while at the same time seeing, for the first time, places and things which escaped them during their visit. Here are works of art hung in obscure, dimly-lit corners, treasures which have been buried under dust allowed to accumulate for untold decades. Some are kept in chambers accessible only by special permission; the Holy of Holies in Bethlehem's Church of the Nativity, and St. Constantin and St. Helena, the Church of the Greek Orthodox Patriarchate, in Jerusalem, are but two examples.

Considerable difficulty was encountered in photographing these works. The Church of the Nativity, for example, is the common property of the Roman Catholic, Greek Orthodox, and Armenian Orthodox churches. Nothing may be touched or moved without the presence of delegates from all three denominations. Permits from high-ranking church officials in Jerusalem were presented to the monks of Bethlehem, but the good friars were nevertheless apprehensive. They watched suspiciously as we removed the icons in the Grotto of the Nativity. We carefully cleared away the layers of dust, removed the glass frames, polished them with oil, and exposed the masterpieces to the camera's lens. The monks' apprehension gave way to keen interest as they saw the art works for the first time in their true glory.

As a matter of fact, the majority of the photographs in this book are of works which have never before been reproduced. This is particularly true of a group of icons found on the altar wall of the Greek Golgotha Chapel in the Church of the Holy Sepulchre. These icons are covered by silver reliefs with openings through which can be seen only the faces, hands and feet of the painted figures. On an evening free of divine service, armed with special permission from Archbishop Basilius, we removed the paintings in order to photograph them. Bishop Danie, curator of the Church, watched us, taking inventory not only of the paintings, but of their artistic content: in his thirty years in Jerusalem, this was the first time he had seen them. Indeed, it may well have been the first time anyone has seen them since the silver covers were set in place.

Most churches in Jerusalem are devoid of the old icons. Much has been lost to plunderers who conquered the Holy Land through the centuries. Objects of art which are particularly valuable are now under lock and key in convents or have found their way to the world's great museums.

The works which we have photographed are an integral part of the holy places and it is our hope that they, together with the sites themselves, combine to present not merely the story, but the mood and the spirit of the Passion, which is, after all, at the heart of this effort.

The question inevitably arises: does such an effort serve a religious purpose? The New Testament entreats its readers to love and respect Jesus. It does not exact tribute to places of meditation in His name, but rather requires that Christians prove their devotion to Jesus by conducting their lives in the spirit of His teachings.

The Gospel According to John says: "Blessed are they that have not seen and yet have believed" (20:29). In this case, then, seeing is not believing. Neither an in-person pilgrimage nor this book can inspire faith in Jesus or imbue the Christian ethic. Hopefully, our work will bolster that faith and enhance that ethic. If so, our purpose has been accomplished.

TABLE OF CONTENTS

I. Background

Foreword 5
The History of the Easter Feast 13
    Chronology 13
    The Name 13
    The Historical Development of Easter 14
    Meaning and Significance of Easter 16

The Holy Places of the Passion 19
    The Holy Places 19
    Uncertainties of Tradition 20
    The Holy Sepulchre 22
    Gethsemane 24
    The Upper Room: The Chamber of the Last Supper 25
    The Palace of Caiaphas 26
    The Praetorium 27
    The Way of the Cross 30

II. Illustrated Section

Entry into Jerusalem 34
They Welcomed Jesus 36
Jesus in the Temple 38
The Plot 40
Preparation for the Supper 42
The Last Supper 44
The Footwashing 48
Gethsemane 50
Gethsemane Prayer 52
The Betrayal 58
Jesus Before the High Priest 62
Peter's Denial 64
Jesus Before Caiaphas 66
The Death of Judas 68
The Trial of Jesus 72
Jesus Before Pilate 76
Release of a Prisoner at the Passover 80
Jesus Before Herod 84
Torturing of Jesus 88
The Shout to Crucify 90
Jesus or Caesar 92
Pilate Washing his Hands 94
On the Way to the Cross 96
Crucifixion 108
Casting Lots Over the Garment 110
Prayer of One of the Thieves 116
The Beloved Disciple 120
The Last Cry from the Cross 124
The Death of Jesus 128
Anointing of Jesus' Body 132
The Tomb of Jesus 138
The Empty Tomb 142
The Risen Lord 150
Doubting Thomas 152

A stone in the Franciscan Church, Bethphage, which stands behind the Mount of Olives. Since the fourth century this has been traditionally known as the place where Mary, the sister of Lazarus, met Jesus. Since medieval times it has also been traditionally known as the place from which Jesus mounted the ass upon which He rode into Jerusalem. Since the time of the Crusader kings there has been a tradition of worshipers going in a procession from this stone to Jerusalem, following the route of Jesus. This tradition was interrupted only during the era of Turkish rule.

The Fresco from the 12th century shows men with palm branches in their hands.

THE HISTORY OF THE EASTER FEAST

Chronology

In the church calendar, Easter Sunday is the fixed point of reference from which the dates of all the other movable feasts are determined. Easter always occurs on the first Sunday following the first full moon of spring, at some time between March 22nd and April 25th. This was not always the case. In the first two centuries A.D., in Asia Minor, Christians celebrated Easter on the third day after the first full moon of spring, regardless of the day of the week on which this occurred. This calculation is based on the Jewish Passover. The Jewish month consists of one lunar phase, beginning and ending with the new moon. The full moon, therefore, occurs on the fourteenth of the month. The fourteenth Nisan is Passover. According to the Gospels of Matthew, Mark and Luke the Last Supper took place on Passover Eve and the Resurrection three days later. For this reason, Easter was celebrated independently of any particular weekday. The followers of this form of calculation were called the "Quartodecimans" (Quartodecimus—14; 14 Nisan—Passover). The Christian communities under Rome's leadership, however, celebrated Easter on Sunday, the day on which the Resurrection took place. In the second century, this resulted in the Easter Dispute which was settled only after the Council of Nicea (325). However, some Quartodecimans retained their method of calculation until the fifth century. As a result of the agreements at Nicea, the Alexandrian Bishops were officially commissioned to announce the Sunday on which Easter should fall. This they had already done on their own in the third century through the sending of Easter letters.

Because of the different calendars, however, the Easter Sundays of the Roman Church still did not correspond to those of the Alexandrian Church. The Roman calendar was based on a cycle in which Easter Sunday fell on the same date every 84 years, while according to the Alexandrian calendar, the cycle lasted only 19 years.

The Alexandrian calendar was first introduced in Rome by Dionysius Exiguus (500-545). It is still observed today by the Catholic and the Protestant Churches.

The Name

While the date of Easter has a biblical basis, the same cannot always be said about the name of the holiday. The German *Ostern* and the English *Easter* have their origins in Ostara, the Germanic Goddess of Earth and Spring. The French *Paques* and the Italian and Spanish *Pascua* stem, however, from the ecclesiastical Latin *Pascha*, which in turn goes back to the Hebrew *Passah*. It is the holiday on which the Last Supper took place, and on which the Paschal lamb was offered.*

---

*After the destruction of the Temple in 70 A.D., no sacrificial lamb was slaughtered except in the Samaritan congregation and by the *Falasha* in Ethiopia.

The relationship between Easter and Passover can be found in the Bible. The Evangelists, with the exception of John, agree that the Last Supper was the meal of the Jewish Passover, and that Jesus was crucified the following day, Friday, and that He arose from the dead in the time period between Saturday night and Sunday morning. John offers an even closer connection. According to John, Jesus died at the same hour in which the Passover lamb was slaughtered at the Temple; in other words, Christ Himself is the sacrificial lamb.

The Historical Development of Easter

The central importance of Easter has from the earliest times been underlined by the length and importance of the liturgical season leading up to it. The duration of Lent was subject to continual evolution. In the second century, worshippers fasted only on Good Friday and Holy Saturday. But in the following century, Lent was extended to all of Holy Week. In 337, following Constantine's death, 36 days were set aside for fasting. In 604, a custom originating in Rome became widespread and Ash Wednesday became the beginning of a forty-day Lent; thus the word *Quadragesima* (Latin: fortieth) was introduced. The period of forty days had sacred significance. The Great Flood of Noah, sent by God to punish man for his sins, lasted forty days. And the Children of Israel were forced to wander in the desert for forty years as atonement for their sins. Moses, Elijah and Christ waited forty days for God's appearance. The purpose of these forty days of fasting is the putting aside of sinful existence and a transition into a new, pure form of life.

Since the Second Vatican Council the days of Quadragesima are no longer regarded by the Roman Catholic Church as days of fasting. Attention is now centered on Holy Week itself. But Ash Wednesday still marks the official commencement of Lent.

Ash Wednesday is named for the symbolic acts of the priests, who burn the palm and olive branches which were blessed on Palm Sunday of the previous year, thus completing the annual cycle. This custom originated in the tenth century. The ashes are sprinkled with holy water and sprayed with incense. This symbolizes life's temporality. With the ashes, the priest marks a small cross on the forehead of the worshipper. (In earlier times, this ceremony was reserved for the penitent.) This mark serves to remind the congregation of the transitory nature of life and calls upon the worshippers to do penance. In the Anglican Church a series of denunciations against sinners and penitential prayers are read; in the Protestant Episcopal Church in the United States only the penitential prayers are read.

Palm Sunday marks the beginning of Holy Week, the last week of Lent, and the one with the oldest and most meaningful of all Christian holidays. On this day, palm branches are blessed in both Catholic and Protestant churches.

Certainly since the fourth century, and perhaps earlier, Holy (Maundy) Thursday has been devoted to the memory of the Last Supper. In the Roman Catholic Church the washing of the feet is then performed as a reenactment of Christ's washing the disciples' feet. The celebrant at the Mass removes his vestments and washes the feet of twelve worshippers. On the same day, the Holy Sacraments are removed from the altars.

North African congregations have celebrated Good Friday as a day of fasting since the second century, but it was only in the fourth century that Good Friday gained its prominent position as the day of the crucifixion. From the writings of the pilgrim nun Egeria*, we learn that on the night of Good Friday there was a Mass at the Stations of the Cross in which the Christians traced the path of Jesus to Golgotha.**

Their pilgrimage led them to all the Stations at which, according to the Gospels, Christ had stopped during the days of His arrest and crucifixion. Starting with the Mount of Olives and the Garden of Gethsemane, they visited the court where Christ was tried, the house of Pontius Pilate and the Via Dolorosa. The procession ended at Christ's grave near Golgotha. Today, the Franciscan Minorite Fathers conduct a procession *every* Friday, beginning at the court house and passing almost the same stations. In the fourth century, worshippers sang antiphonies on their way to the grave, and the Gospels describing Christ's Passion were read. Next morning, additional Bible passages were read at the grave. The Adoration of the Cross took place from the sixth to the ninth hour*** (from twelve noon to three o'clock in the afternoon), the hours of death. The service concluded with the reading of the Gospel According to John.

In the antiphonies, the three women**** and the angel at Christ's grave were represented by priests. Obviously, this was an attempt to depict the events of Easter Sunday. The antiphonal reading of the Gospels of the Passion, the reading of the Passion According to John during the Good Friday Mass, and the Adoration of the Cross, later became part of the Roman Liturgy.

At one time, Easter was the only Christian holiday. Thus, the Easter Vigil is the oldest of all vigils. Observed since the second century, it is still, today, the high point of the Easter celebration in many churches. In the fourth century, it was officially celebrated on Sunday morning. Four hundred years later, however, it was changed to the Saturday afternoon before Easter, and then to that morning. The Eastern Orthodox churches have always retained the Vigil on the night of Easter Eve, and this has once again become the Roman Catholic usage by an edict of Pope Pius XII.

The Easter Vigil still holds its place in today's Roman liturgy. In earlier times, baptism was performed only once a year and was closely connected with the Easter Vigil. Since about the fifth century children have been baptized throughout the year, and at the Easter Vigil an act of symbolic rebaptism has been held, in which the worshipper is required to profess his faith anew through the performance of an act of penitence before the entire congregation.

Meaning and Significance of Easter

The purpose of Lent and Easter is to bring about a thorough renewal of man. Clear evidence of this can be seen on Ash Wednesday: The old and sinful is reduced to ashes and man is summoned to repentance in order to experience the beginning of a new and happier time.

The first Easter customs have their roots in this idea of the end of one period and the beginning of another. In the oldest Christian communities, Sunday was considered the first day of the week. This was why the congregation of Corinth (1. Cor. 16 : 2) assembled each Sunday. The underlying thought is closely related to Easter: Sunday is the day of the Resurrection, the new beginning.

Shortly thereafter, the Christian congregations in Jerusalem observed the yearly Easter which then fell on the third day after the Jewish Passover Eve. The annual Easter holiday was the church's New Year holiday.

From its earliest origins, the Easter Eve ceremony has been preceded by a fast, as, for example, in the case of the Quartodecimans who fasted on the 15th of Nisan, the day after the Last Supper, which corresponds to Good Friday. They did this not because of Christ's death but as atonement for those Jews who had not accepted Christ. Christ, coming from the world of sinners, suffers during the Passion for the sins of that world, dies and rises again to a new life, a life of salvation. He brings mankind into a new world, into the world of Christianity. It was because of the correspondence between this and the symbolism of baptism that baptisms took place only on Easter. The heathen neophytes fasted forty days but not in mourning for the death of Christ, as was later explained. Rather, they fasted to prepare themselves spiritually for their death *with* Christ; it was their personal passion. On Good Friday, they died with Christ and through baptism rose again from the dead with Him to a new Christian life.

As we have seen, the forty days served not only to purify and prepare the Christian converts but also to cleanse the penitents of the Old Testament. The sacramental Easter Communion, in which the preparation of the neophyte for God reaches its conclusion, also reflects a Jewish tradition. According to John, Christ was nailed to the Cross during the same hour that the sacrificial lamb was slaughtered in the Temple. In other words, He died as the sacrificial lamb; Christ Himself is the sacrifice (John 18 : 28; 19 : 14).

In Jewish tradition, the blood of the sacrificial lamb is poured in God's presence.* In the temple, it was poured before the sacrificial altar and thus was an offering to God. At the same time, it had a cleansing effect on those making the offering. Should the offering then be consumed, one could consider oneself to be God's guest. Similar ideas prevail in the Communion.

The communicants are guests of God at the feast of Passover; that is, the Last Supper. (Mark 14 : 12-14; Luke 22 : 15). Jesus Christ lives with and within the faithful, but they remove themselves from Him by their sins, and so must repent in order to be re-established in the Christian community. For this reason, Lent is a time of fasting.

Two ideas are therefore closely related to Lent:

1. The neophyte dies with Jesus, is buried with Him (Romans 6 : 4) and rises again from the dead with Him. One finds in the baptism a re-enactment of Jesus' death and resurrection (Romans 6 : 5).
2. The penitent dies with Jesus in order to rise with Him free of sin.

It is not only baptism which is closely connected with the "new beginning" of Easter. The desire to separate oneself from the sinful past and to enter into a new and better existence is reflected in the Christian wish for healing. Once again, this has a paschal basis with its roots in ancient Jewish beliefs.

The Jews recognize four Passover events. The first is the covenant between Abraham and Jehovah. It is a covenant in blood, ratified by circumcision.*

The second Passover event—the second blood covenant—is the sacrifice of Isaac by his father Abraham. The father is called upon to sacrifice his son. (The son is made to carry the wood of his own sacrificial fire just as Jesus was forced to carry His own cross.) The third Passover event, the Exodus, is the best known. On the night when the first-born children of the Egyptians were killed, the Jews, in order to save their own children, marked their houses with the blood of a sacrificial lamb. This is the night before the Exodus, the Passover night. The slaughtered lamb is

*In Egypt, for example, the angel of vengeance passed over those portals that were smeared with blood.

**Brit abraham abinu, "the union of our father Abraham," is the Hebrew synonym for circumcision.

the Passover lamb. The fourth and last Passover event is closely connected to chiliastic ideas. It will be the last night before Judgement Day on which the Messiah will come and the world will be saved. This belief predates Christianity. In the Septuagint* Jeremiah 31 : 3 is translated: "In the feast of the Passover I will unite them [the Children of Israel] from the ends of the earth."

The Crucifixion of Christ forms a continuation in the chain of Passover events. As the supreme sacrifice, God now offers His begotten Son.

With this offer, a new covenant replaces the one concluded between God and Noah, representing all mankind, after the first Day of Judgement or the Great Flood.

According to Jewish belief, Judgement Day will resemble the Great Flood. All sinners will be destroyed and a new 1000-year epoch will begin with the appearance of the Messiah. Christians believe that Jesus Christ will return to earth on Judgement Day as the final Judge to establish a new realm of Paradise on earth.

*The translation of the Old Testament from the Hebrew into Greek which was commissioned by Ptolemy II Philadelphos in 250 B.C. and written by the Jews.

THE HOLY PLACES OF THE PASSION
Spiritual Value of the Holy Places and Pilgrimage

The Holy Places

Why "holy?" And why visit them? Because as humans we are sensitive, knowing and loving through our bodies, and because God deigned to place Himself within reach of our senses, meeting us even in our own flesh. That is the Incarnation: the Son of God taking a slave's condition and becoming like all men (Philippians 2:7). He walked on our paths, gazed on our landscapes, breathed our air, withstood our heat and our cold, in that country of Palestine, that city of Jerusalem, which He chose above all others. For us to go there now and walk around is to find Him again, know His joys, share His weariness, hear Him repeat to us the love of His Father through the simple and strong words of His Aramaic dialect . . . parables so very fresh, flavored with the land of Palestine. It is the Gospel itself that sings again when we listen throughout these lands where it took its birth. Behind it: the whole Bible, preparing, surrounding, expanding the Gospel—that story which God enacted with man, with all men, communing with them in place and time. Emmanuel: "God with us." There is the wonder of the Bible's revelation, which distinguishes it from all others. It is not a body of abstract doctrines, not a philosophical system like so many others, but the real and living movement of a Father Who came to speak to His children in their language and walk with them along their paths in the person of His Son.

The veneration of the Holy Places is far from superstitious or magical. It is not the worship of stone or monument. It is the search for God Himself, His Word and His Love, through the physical contacts which He offers voluntarily to our sense-directed natures, in order to take us completely as we are, touching our souls through our bodies. He "placed himself in our skin". "Philip, He who seeth me seeth the Father" (John 14:9). Of course God is Spirit and the "true worshippers worship the Father in spirit and truth" (John 4:23). Everywhere in the world and across every century He has let Himself be found by those who believe in Him and love Him. But He has tried to give tangible expressions to His Word and Love, and He urges His children to use these things, in order to infuse their daily lives with His presence.

It is this sense awareness which makes the pilgrimage so precious. This return to the sources acts upon us like an elixir. That "holy tale" which I studied in schoolbooks, which goes back to my childhood memories, a beautiful distant Middle Eastern legend, suddenly becomes a real history, something near to me with dimensions I can grasp. It really happened somewhere, it happened here in places I can visit over and over. These landscapes, made famous through the skill of the great painters, have thereby always seemed imaginary and somewhat fantastic. Now

I learn to know them in their simpler, raw reality, and now how much more close they seem.

This striking contact revives my awareness and my faith. A book has been written with the title "The Sacrament of Jerusalem." Certainly not a sacrament in the proper or sublime sense of the act or of the physical element which, in any point in time or space, allows me to touch by faith the Risen Body of Christ. But a sacrament just the same as a sensible means of helping me to find the precious presence of the One Who willed to live among us, as one of us. In Jerusalem the faith of the Christian feels Jesus Christ to be closer. The horizons He looked at, the streets that retrace the very ways He followed, the monuments that recall His memory, these very icons in which the brethren of old attempted to express their faith and love ... all that recalls for me His person, His action and message—an immediate contact of inestimable value. I am more aware that He lived my human life and I feel strengthened to walk in His footsteps.

But this was a life of humiliation and privation. The lesson of the Holy Places is in many ways a lesson in humility. First because it indicates more readily the humble and limited dimensions God and His Son took to reach me in all my mediocrity. Palestine is a tiny country. Jerusalem is a small city. The pilgrim is struck by this from the very first: This is not at all like the great spaces of the distant lands he comes from, or like the splendor of modern cities. Five miles from Jerusalem to Bethlehem; ninety-three miles from Jerusalem to Nazareth: the size of a very ordinary province. And even at the time of Jesus, or before Him at the time of the Prophets, it was truly a small, almost negligible country beside the great empires of Egypt and Assyria, with a culture much less developed than that of Greece or Rome. Still, it is in this country that God chose to appear, precisely because it was small and backward, so that the sublime quality of the Revelation cannot be attributed to the wisdom or power of men. Times have changed, but the country has remained unpretentious. The people who appear, indifferent or uncaring, jeering, at the pilgrim's Way of the Cross in the lanes of Jerusalem, are probably much like those who once saw the poor Galilean pass by, bearing His Cross toward Calvary. "Being found in form as a man, He humbled himself, and became obedient unto death, even the death of the cross." (Philippians 2:7-8) Galilee is humble and joyful; Jerusalem is humble but mournful. Mournful but also glorious, because it is there that the extreme humiliation was consummated in triumph. "Wherefore God also hath highly exalted him, and given him a name which is above every name: that at the name of Jesus every knee should bow, of things in heaven, and things in earth, and things under the earth; and that every tongue should confess that Jesus Christ is Lord, to the glory of God the Father." (Philippians 2:9-11)

Uncertainties of Tradition

What has man done to this glory? There, even now, Jerusalem teaches its lesson of humility and privation. The pilgrim is naturally shocked by the condition of the Holy Places: certain sites have been forgotten and can no longer be pointed out without the purest fantasy; others are uncertain and in question; even the surest ones are disputed by different Christian confessions; and they are covered by monuments whose purposes may have been commendable to be sure but whose existence cannot allow us to overlook the shabby state of these sites, or their poor art. God has allowed the meanness and sin of men to damage the souvenirs of His presence which He has left behind. It is a process of abasement inaugurated by the Incarnation. If the Son was misunderstood, tortured, and cruelly treated, can one hope for more with the material remains of His passage among us, a world of sinners? Here we must submit. The ways of God are not our ways; it is not without design that He lets His work of salvation be exposed to both the spiritual and tangible unseemliness of sin. His utter compliance gives us a lesson of humility, of stripping bare. He shows us how not to attach too great an importance to scientific certitude or to aesthetic emotions. Faith can use the tangible evidence but it goes far beyond it and must know how to free itself from it. To visit these places as an aesthete, the way a Pierre Loti did, can lead only to disappointment. The pilgrim must overcome the shock at the disputes and the base actions of men through a purified faith that pursues the essential question: the finding of Jesus Christ Who actually hallowed these places, no matter what men have been able to do with them.

However one must pierce through to the essential and not be too easily disheartened. It is as sad to accept without analysis every site noted by all-too-clever guides, as it would be regrettable to put everything in doubt and go away a sceptic, saying that all is false and that we no longer know anything. Indeed, we do know something, a great deal in fact. But a serious and critical examination is necessary to untangle the true from the false, the probable from the improbable, and to perceive in each case the degree of certainty attainable. It will never be absolute certitude, because history is not metaphysics, still less the certainty of faith, because faith is not involved in this type of decision. But it is a historical certainty all the same, which, based on an objective study of the sources, can guarantee a certain kernel of solid conviction. Now, this kernel of conviction is substantial and fortunately extends to all the sites of major interest. Let us consider it in terms of the Passion.

It is not surprising that many minor elements have been lost or obscured. The first community of Jerusalem, weak and persecuted, had other preoccupations than the cataloguing for the future of the places already familiar to it. They were all absorbed with the presence of the Risen Lord, living among His own. They met around brotherly tables where the remembrance of the Word and the "breaking of bread" brought the Master to them. The community's structure developed, little by little. Its members cared little for future centuries, because they were awaiting the imminent return of the glorious Lord. Such an atmosphere was hardly suited to the conscious preservation of traditions to act as guides for twentieth-century pilgrims. There could be no question of that, nor of building monuments on every hallowed spot. We understand under these conditions that many sites of secondary interest have vanished from memory, owing to a lack of written or architectural data.

The Holy Sepulchre

But major souvenirs could not be easily erased from memory. The first in importance were the Cross and the tomb of the Master—touching truly the center of the faith. The death and resurrection of Jesus were the basis of the early teachings of which some samples have been preserved for us in the speeches of Peter in the *Acts of the Apostles*. The Christians of Jerusalem could not forget the sacred spot, hallowed above all others, where the redemption of the world was accomplished. Now there were always Christians in Jerusalem. An obscure minority to be sure, but a living community whose leaders are known to us. These Christians were to point out from father to son the location of Calvary and the Tomb. They were not interested in surrounding them with churches. Besides, the Jews and the Romans would never have allowed it. The Romans even constructed the Forum at Calvary after 135, for their new foundation "Aelia Capitolina". But even this contributed to making the memory more concrete. By placing the Forum on this spot, Emperor Hadrian certainly had no idea of hindering the worship (which he knew nothing about) of an obscure sect he paid no heed to anyway. But he was unwittingly adding a new buttress to the Christian memory. "It is there," one might say from then on, "near the Forum of the Romans, that you find the tomb of our Master." And that is what the Christians of Jerusalem told Emperor Constantine, once he had become a Christian himself, when he sought to honor the site of the redemption. A search confirmed the tradition as it was thus preserved: according to contemporary Eusebius of Caesarea, these searches disclosed the tomb of Jesus and, close by, the site of the Crucifixion. There the Christian Emperor and his mother Helena built in 326 a magnificent group of structures, of which the present Holy Sepulchre is the humble but faithful successor.

Its location within the city astonishes only those visitors with peripheral knowledge of the subject. Archaeological work has proved that the ramparts of the city in the time of Jesus passed further south (under the present Lutheran church), then eastward (along the Souq-ez-Zeith), forming a corner with a gate (which can be found in the Alexandrian Hospice of the Russian Sisters) and leaving a space outside of the city where gardens and tombs were once found. A Jewish tomb from the time of the Gospel is still visible at the western end of the Constanti-

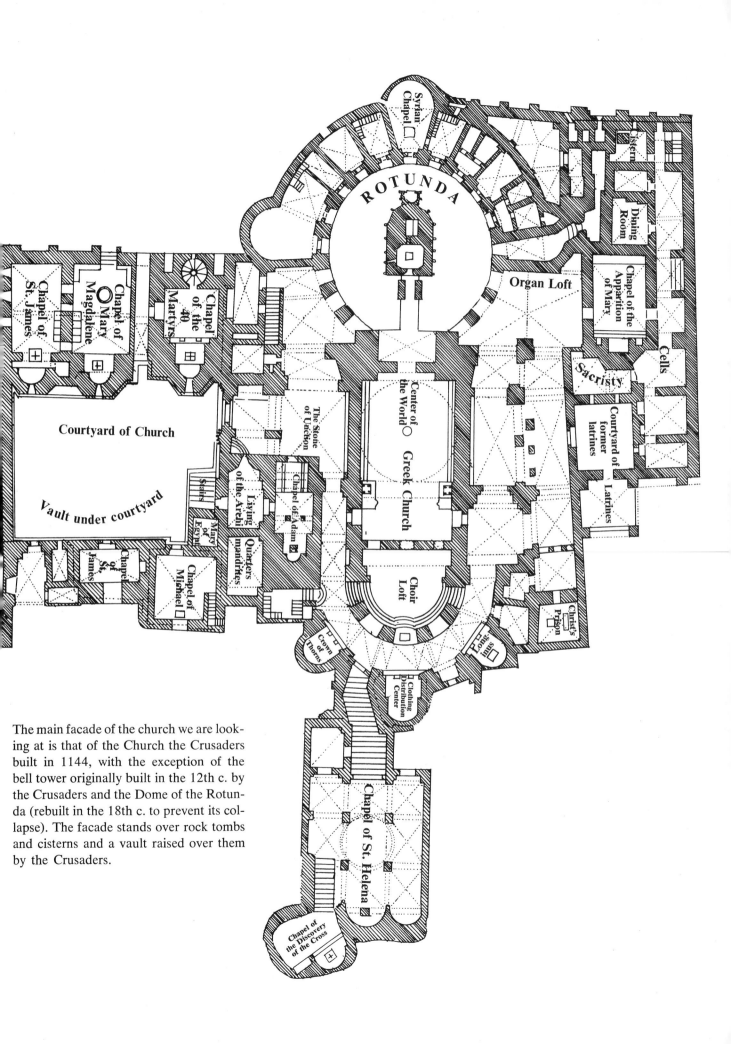

Syrian Chapel

ROTUNDA

Cistern

Dining Room

Organ Loft

Chapel of the Apparition of Mary

Chapel of Mary Magdalene

Chapel of the 40 Martyrs

Chapel of St. James

Cells

Sacristy

Center of the World

Courtyard of former latrines

Courtyard of Church

The Stone of Unction

Greek Church

Latrines

Vault under courtyard

Stairs

Laying Quarters of the Archimandrites

Chapel of Adam

Chapel of St. James

Mary of Egypt

Chapel of Michael

Choir Loft

Christ's Prison

Crown of Thorns

Longinus

Clothing Distribution Center

Chapel of St. Helena

Chapel of the Discovery of the Cross

The main facade of the church we are looking at is that of the Church the Crusaders built in 1144, with the exception of the bell tower originally built in the 12th c. by the Crusaders and the Dome of the Rotunda (rebuilt in the 18th c. to prevent its collapse). The facade stands over rock tombs and cisterns and a vault raised over them by the Crusaders.

nian Rotunda. It was on a rocky outcrop in this area, near the rampart, beside the major road to the sea, that the condemned were crucified. There, in a private tomb belonging to Joseph of Arimathaea, Jesus was laid in His shroud. All that is perfectly probable, and no other spot in Jerusalem can offer locations as likely to be authentic as this traditional one; least of all the "Garden Tomb" where pilgrims are taken just to see a Byzantine tomb thought by General Gordon to be the tomb of Christ.

Constantine's monument has suffered greatly through the centuries. After several destructions had been repaired, the great church that extended eastward above the grotto where piety celebrated the finding of the Cross was completely destroyed by the Caliph Hakim in 1009. The tomb itself was then demolished with axes. Only the Constantinian rotunda survived almost intact. The Crusades preserved it, and, between 1099 and 1149, added to it a Romanesque church that extends to the east. It is this monument, a composite of Byzantine and Medieval, that has lasted down to our day. Once harmonious and clean of line, it has suffered the wounds of time, especially the ravages of a great fire in 1808. But the restoration presently in progress has already given it back much of its original beauty, and we can hope that an intelligent cooperation of the responsible communities will finally succeed in restoring its original appearance, which is not only beautiful but precious because of its long history. Across sixteen centuries of seething change, the tradition of the fourth century is still found embedded within it, and we have seen that this tradition has every possibility of going back to the time of the Gospel. So, when the pilgrim kneels at the foot of the Cross or before the Tomb, if he will only close his eyes to the finery and his ears to the noise, his faith enters into a physical and living contact with the Event that saved the world.

Gethsemane

At the beginning of the Passion account, another Holy Place is cited: the garden of Gethsemane, in which Jesus felt the agony of His imminent death. The Mount of Olives has not moved. Olive trees are found at its foot and on its slopes. Everything agrees with the spot indicated by the Gospels. Besides, a Christian church built by Theodosius the Great consecrated the place from the end of the fourth century onward. This church, sacked by the Persians in 614 and replaced in the Middle Ages by a slightly altered one was found and reconstructed at the beginning of this century by the Franciscans. The interior with its rich finishings and dim light creates an atmosphere which brings to bear upon the pilgrim the very feeling of the supreme test of the Master. The rock slab before the High Altar need not represent the exact spot where Jesus sweated blood. We can equally challenge the merits of this church and a neighboring grotto respectively to preserve the precise memory of either the agony or the betrayal, because these locations have varied through the ages. Finally, the old olive trees, which stand in a garden, which is perhaps a bit too neatly kept, can only be the children or the grandchildren of those which gave shelter to the sadness of that tragic night. These hesitations concerning details in no way detract from the essential value of this site as the theater for the stirring drama where the love of Jesus for this sinful world triumphed over His human anguish.

The Upper Room: The Chamber of the Last Supper

Moving to earlier in the night of the Passion, can we identify the room where Jesus celebrated the Last Supper? The spot in the southwest of the city, venerated today as the "Cenacle," goes back deep into antiquity. There, between 340 and 345 a great church was constructed, called by Cyril of Jerusalem the "Upper Church of the Apostles." It would soon receive the additional titles of "Holy Sion" and "Mother of All Churches." It is known that this church superseded a smaller, but much more ancient church which marked the location of the Upper Room where the Risen Christ appeared to the Apostles; here they received the Holy Spirit and afterwards held their meetings. This was the cradle of the primitive community and the seat of the Bishop of Jerusalem down to the day when the Holy Sepulchre was built. This tradition, well supported by ancient witnesses, is very plausible and even probable. Despite recent archaeological work on this hill from which no firm conclusions can be drawn, it does seem that this southern extension of the western hill of Jerusalem was inhabited in the time of the Gospel. There stood the palace of the High Priests; in any case, the Byzantine tradition is unanimous in placing there the spot where Christians assembled from the very beginning of the Church.

This tradition, it must be admitted, is much firmer in associating the event of Pentecost with this site rather than the Last Supper. The site of the Last Supper was believed, until the sixth century, to have been in the grotto of Eleona, at the top of the Mount of Olives, or in Gethsemane. Such locations, often the result of ceremonial liturgies, are topographically unsuitable: Jesus must have celebrated His Paschal meal inside the town, according to the law. It would be natural that this upper room, chosen for His last meeting, filled with such precious memories, would be the very room to which the disciples would later return, to receive the Holy Spirit. The pilgrim can thus visit this hallowed spot with solid probability when he visits the remains of that church which has been ruined since the thirteenth century, either in the medieval oratory acquired by the Franciscans in the fourteenth century and converted into a mosque in the sixteenth, or in the neighboring church recently built by German Benedictines, partially recovering the location of the old church, and commemorating the Dormition of the Virgin Mary, which was also associated with this site.

So when he wanders toward Gethsemane, along the path that slopes down the west side of the Tyropoeon Valley on the property of the Assumptionist Fathers, the pilgrim can say he is retracing the path followed by Jesus when He left the room after the Last Supper, after the chanting of the Hallel,* to go and face His arrest, trial, and death. This route certainly follows one of the old winding streets of the old city and, in following it, we are walking in the very footsteps of Jesus. Today, as of old, it leads toward the Kidron, which the Master Himself must have crossed, passing on His right the picturesque old tombs said to be those of Absalom and Zachariah, which were in existence in His time and whose weird silhouettes still rise against the full moon as they did on the first Easter.

The Palace of Caiaphas

Between Gethsemane and Calvary the route of the Passion grows more uncertain. The two principal points, the Palace of the High Priest and the Praetorium of Pilate, are greatly in dispute.

Concerning the former, we must first clear up one ambiguity. The pilgrims of old venerated at the Palace of Caiaphas the Flagellation of Jesus, the Crowning with Thorns, and even His imprisonment. The Gospels say no such thing: they mention neither prison nor flagellation, the latter being placed, according to them, in the Roman praetorium. They do say that Jesus spent the night in the palace of the High Priest, but it is not even sure if that High Priest was Caiaphas, and still less certain that any judicial meeting was held during the night. Actually, their indications do not agree, and we must choose from them. A complete critical examination, which cannot be developed fully in this text, allows us to reconstruct the succession of events. After His arrest in Gethsemane, Jesus is led to the house of Annas (John 18 : 13), a former High Priest (Luke 3 : 2; Acts of the Apostles 4 : 6). There a brief interrogation takes place, ending with Jesus' being struck in the face (John 18 : 19-23), followed by outrages on the part of the guards who jeer at Jesus and make sport of Him (Luke 22 : 63-65). During this time, in the courtyard where Jesus is mocked, Peter denies His Master and draws from Him that glance that strikes so deeply (Luke 22 : 54-62). It is not until the very early dawn that Jesus is led before Caiaphas (John 18 : 24), in the building of the Sanhedrin (Luke 22 : 66) where a single rapid meeting lists the grievances and the requested sentence that will be brought before Pilate (Luke 22: 67 ; 23 : 7). Matthew and Mark seem to place this meeting sometime during the night (Matthew 26 : 59-66; Mark 14 : 55-64), distinguishing it from another meeting in the morning about which they say nothing (Matthew 27 : 1, Mark 15 : 1); and only Matthew specifies that this night convocation took place in the house of Caiaphas (Matthew 26 : 57). There is much confusion here: trials were never held at night in Israel, and the normal place for a trial was not in the house of the High Priest but in the building of the Sanhedrin, which overlapped the sacred territory of the Temple, toward the southwest of the present day Haram esh-Sherif.

*The cycle of Psalms, 113-118, used by Jews in the Passover liturgy.

Once this is made clear, we can try to locate the palace of the High Priest (Annas) which an unquestioning tradition has called the "palace of Caiaphas," in which Jesus spent the night preceding His judgment. The most ancient tradition is rather firm in its location on the southern esplanade of the western hill, a little to the north of the Chamber of the Last Supper; it accepted this proximity and sought to justify it in different ways. It seems clear from certain texts that a basilica bearing the name of "Saint Peter" was built there around the end of the fifth or beginning of the sixth century. Though there has been no systematic research, some archaeological remains allow a location in the Armenian area called "Holy Saviour" between the southern rampart of the city and the church of the Dormition, slightly north of an oratory which succeeded it in the fifteenth century. Such a site is not unlikely: this southern esplanade of the western hill offered beautiful space for buildings, and we can understand how a family of High Priests could have established residence on it.

A recent opinion, however, claims to locate the palace of Caiaphas elsewhere: on the eastern slope of the hill leading down to Siloam. Careful excavations by the Assumptionist Fathers have revealed an ancient sanctuary constructed above a deep grotto. The fortunate possessors of these ruins have tried to present them as the ancient Church of "Saint Peter" built on the location of the palace of Caiaphas: the grotto would have been revered as a site of the prison of Christ and one would see near it a scourging place. But this account seems to be based on some confusion. An ancient church was there, whose remains date back to the fifth and sixth centuries. But it is more likely another sanctuary, recognized also by tradition, likewise dedicated to the memory of Saint Peter, more precisely to his repentance. In this "St. Peter in Gallicantu" was commemorated the spot where the Apostle was supposed to have fled to weep over his denial of the Master. The grotto, marked with the painted crosses of worshippers of old, fits very well the recollections of pilgrims. It makes no claim to be a prison where Jesus was incarcerated and the building which rose above it could not have been the palace of Caiaphas, which we must still seek on the more favorable and traditional site at the top of the hill. It is from this latter place on the morning of Good Friday that Jesus was most likely led to the Sanhedrin, then to the Court of Pilate. But where was the Praetorium?

The Praetorium

Here again we find uncertainty and dispute. Tradition is particularly weak and hesitant on this point. The successive locations represent less real recollections than pure conjecture, based on theological considerations, or simple inventions drawn from handy ruins. In the Byzantine era, the Praetorium or "Santa Sophia" (Holy Wisdom), as it was then called, was sought in the Tyropoeon Valley, somewhat west of the Temple esplanade, either to the north in the place which later became the church of the "Spasm", (of Mary), which today belongs to the Armenian Catholics or rather to the south near Bab es-Silsileh, where the Turkish Tribunal (Mehkemeh) once stood. This corresponds approximately to the location of the ancient Jewish Sanhedrin, and it is quite possible that the appearance of Jesus before the authorities of His people attracted to this area the memory of His appearance before Pilate. At the end of the Byzantine Era, probably because the Moslem invasion and possession of the Temple forbade open Christian worship in these places, this location disappears. But the memory was transported to two different parts of the city: first on Zion in the southwest, and then in the area stretching north from the Temple.

Since the palace of Caiaphas had already grouped many reminders of the Passion, including a scourging post, and the place of the Crowning with Thorns, it was natural to put the house of Pilate nearer to them. This is what medieval pilgrimage routes did when they placed the house of Pilate near that of Caiaphas, north of the Cenacle. A chapel in the Praetorium, bearing the title "Holy Saviour," was hallowed in this spot until the thirteenth century.

Others preferred to place the Praetorium elsewhere, north of the Temple, on a direct path leading from Gethsemane to the Holy Sepulchre and passing along the Probatic Pool. Other ruins were found there as well, such as those of the Antonia, which were available for the localization of Passion events. The Middle Ages saw the growth and spread of many oratories such as those of the Flagellation and of the Condemnation (still preserved in the Biblical Institute of the Franciscan Fathers) or the Oratory of the "Respite" where Jesus would have been put in prison on His arrival from Gethsemane, and of which something may have been preserved, either in the medieval monument of the Cheikh Derbas in the Moslem school called "Raoudah" (just south of the above-mentioned Franciscan monastery), or in the small structure also from the medieval period, "Koursi Isa" (the seat of Jesus) in the northern part of Haram esh-Sherif. These were pious inventions as was the creation in 1906, in the "Praetorium" of the Greeks adjoining the Ecce Homo, of a "Prison of Christ," obtained by the transformation of an ancient tomb.

Medieval tradition has been preserved to the present particularly in the convent of the Sisters of Our Lady of Zion, where diligent and ably executed excavations purport to have found remains of the Antonia and have unearthed a beautiful ancient pavement which would be the "lithostrotos" of the Gospel (John 19 : 13). This identification poses grave problems, however, historical as well as archaeological. On one hand, it has not been proved that the Roman governor ever had a permanent residence there or that his occasional presence there would have warranted the title of Praetorium for that place. Agreement with Gospel facts is far from perfect, besides, because the lithostroton (the more accurate form of the name) of the Gospel must have been located outside the Praetorium (John 18 : 28-29, 33, 38; 19 : 4-5, 9, 13). But the pavement exhibited here is an interior court. No more is archaeology satisfied with these findings. The restoration, illustrated by ingenious models, rests on very doubtful evidence and extends the Antonia fortress too far to the north and east. It was probably limited to the area occupied by the Moslem school between the street and the Haram. Still more seriously the pavement called "lithostrotos" probably dates only from the second century: it covers up a reservoir which was still uncovered in the time of the siege of the year 70 (cf. Josephus, *Jewish War*, Book V, 476). Recent tests seem to prove that it was conceived and executed at the same time as the Roman arch still partially visible, whose construction can safely be attributed to Hadrian, after 135.

We are therefore led to believe that the Court was located in a place which while unsupported by tradition, is more likely historically: the Palace of Herod rising west of the city, one of whose towers has been preserved under the misnomer "Tower of David," near the Jaffa Gate. There, in the palace of the ancient sovereign according to the custom general in the Empire, the Roman governor resided during his visits to Jerusalem. This is what earned for this residence the permanent title of "Praetorium" or Governor's Palace. We know also from Philo and Josephus that the Procurator of Palestine stayed here when visiting Jerusalem. The danger of rioting in the Temple during feasts which is evoked to justify his provisional residence in the Antonia is unconvincing as an argument. Normally during festivals, the governor went up to Jerusalem from Caesarea, but this was no reason why he should have immured himself in the fortress of Antonia. The one cohort stationed there under a tribune was enough to manage the Temple area, as one can readily see in the case of the Apostle Paul (Acts 21 : 30-36). The governor would indeed have been unwise to establish himself there as well, at the Antonia, and to leave empty the Royal Palace, which, from its high vantage point, controlled the whole western sector of the city.

This then is probably where Pilate was during the Passion, there he judged and condemned Jesus. Excavations cannot be carried out at this spot with the freedom possible at the Antonia, and probably would no longer reveal anything of great value, since this area, traditionally a seat of civic power, has been affected so greatly by the changes of history. Since Herod's time, this part of the city has often been occupied by government or army, the Roman legion in the first centuries of the Christian era, palace of Crusading Kings, Turkish and later Jordanian barracks. All this explains to a great extent why Christian worship has never been able to maintain a firm hold here. Though we lack archaeological evidence, we do have texts wholly in conformity with the topographical evidence of the New Testament passion account; for instance, the account of the seditions under Gessius Florus in 64-66 A.D. (Josephus, *Jewish War*, Book II,

301-308), which depicts the Jewish mob rioting before the Royal Palace and the governor setting soldiers upon the rabble in the "Upper Market," then the prisoners led to his tribunal, whipped and crucified. This tribunal standing in front of the palace must have been a platform of intricately colored tiles that might have been called the "Lithostroton" in the normal technical sense of the word at that time and which, because of its elevation compared to the rest of the city, could have earned for itself the title of Gabbatha (John 10 : 13).

The Way of the Cross

If this be the more probable location of the Praetorium, the Way of the Cross must have differed considerably from the accepted one which goes up from the Antonia toward the Holy Sepulchre.

The probable "Via Dolorosa" must in fact have descended from the Palace of Herod by a road in the opposite direction. Since it was necessary for the condemned man, weighed down by his own cross or at least the cross-bar, to follow the streets to be made an example to the crowd, Jesus must have followed a course close to that of the present David Street, coming down from the "Tower of David," towards the Temple and then the road of the three parallel souks which ends east of Calvary. There, rejoining the present course of the Way of the Cross, He probably crossed that ancient threshold which can still be seen today in the Alexandrian Hospice and remains an authentic place of devotion for worshipping Christians.

Let us not forget that shortly before the condemnation and departure for Calvary, He had made a brief journey from Pilate to Herod and from Herod back to Pilate (Luke 23 : 7-11). This Herod, surnamed Antipas, son of Herod the Great, no longer lived in the palace of his father. The Palace had now become the Roman Praetorium. During his stays in Jerusalem, this Tetrarch of Galilee must have resided in the private family palace, whose location is approximately known: certainly not the "House of Herod" created by medieval imagination between the Antonia and the Probatic Pool (in the place where the present-day Franciscan convent of the Flagellation now stands), but the Hasmonean residence overlooking the Temple, west of the Tyropoeon, across from the Wailing Wall, where synagogues are still standing in the center of the Jewish quarter.

This discussion has, we hope, made clear that all is not of equal certainty concerning the places and routes of the Passion. But neither is all equally jumbled and doubtful. The authenticity of certain points is particularly vulnerable, but others are surer and much more solid. These, happily, are the more important ones, especially the place where Jesus died, was laid to rest, and finally was resurrected. The pilgrim who takes the trouble to study and become informed can follow with assurance the pathways of his Master. This intelligent and honestly founded conviction is a great consolation to him. Again, he must try to transcend a materialistic need for physical contact. Such contact is invaluable because it shocks our senses, but is only worthwhile if it feeds our faith. What matters is to become more aware, as we travel over the roadways of the Holy City, of the concrete and tangible dimensions, both humble and exalting, of the drama of our salvation. Here, the Son of God, a man like me, suffered and died for me. There my Lord rose again for me. In this experience which touches me deeply, in my body as well as in my soul, I find grace to live and die with my Master, in order to rise again with Him. This is the grace of Jerusalem.

Pierre Benoit, O.P.
Jerusalem, February 1968

Queen Helen and her son, Emperor Constantine, with the cross. Helen was the first queen to convert to Christianity. She went to the Holy Land to identify the traditional location of the Holy Places. Among other relics, she unearthed—according to tradition-the Holy Cross. (See caption to the St. Helen Chapel in the Holy Sepulchre).

The illustration shows Helen and Constantine near the Cross after its discovery (390-395). It is in the Armenian parish Church of St. James in Jerusalem. It was made in Armenia and brought to Jerusalem in the 17th Century.

ENTRY INTO JERUSALEM

And when they came nigh to Jerusalem, unto
Bethphage and Bethany, at the mount of Olives,
he sendeth forth two of his disciples, and saith
unto them, Go your way into the village over
against you: and as soon as ye be entered into it,
ye shall find a colt tied, whereon never man sat;
loose him, and bring him. And if any man say
unto you, Why do ye this? say ye that the Lord
hath need of him; and straightway he will send him
hither.

Mark 11:1-3

Jesus' entry into Jerusalem. A
ceramic tile in the Etchmiadzin
chapel in the church of the Armenian Patriarch, St. James.

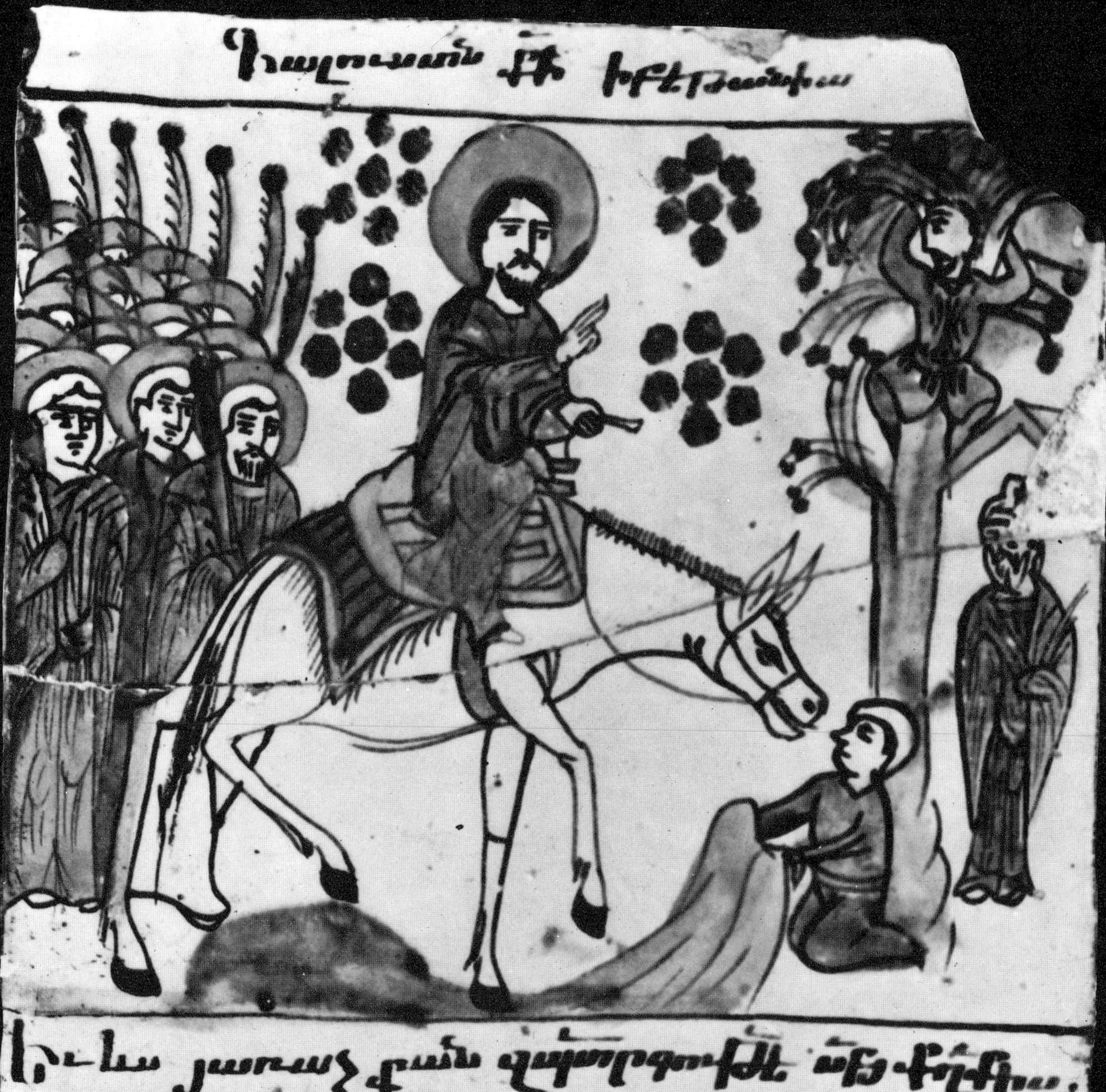

And they that went before, and they that followed, cried, saying, Hosanna; Blessed is he that cometh in the name of the Lord.

THEY WELCOMED JESUS

And they went their way, and found the colt tied by the door without in a place where two ways met; and they loosed him. And certain of them that stood there said unto them, What do ye, loosing the colt? And they said unto them even as Jesus had commanded: and they let them go. And they brought the colt to Jesus, and cast their garments on him; and he sat upon him. And many spread their garments in the way: and others cut down branches off the trees, and strewed them in the way. And they that went before, and they that followed, cried, saying,

Hosanna; Blessed is he that cometh
in the name of the Lord:
Blessed be the kingdom of our father
David, that cometh in the name
of the Lord:
Hosanna in the highest.

Mark 11:4-10

And when the chief priests and scribes saw the wonderful things that he did, and the children crying in the temple, and saying, Hosanna to the son of David; they were sore displeased, and said unto him, Hearest thou what these say? And Jesus saith unto them, Yea; have ye never read, Out of the mouth of babes and sucklings thou hast perfected praise? *Matt. 21:15-16*

Jesus entering Jerusalem. The old Greek inscription on the top says, "The Palm Branch Tribute," and the inscription at the bottom says, "Hosanna, to the son of David, Blessed be he who comes in the name of the Lord, Hosanna in the highest."

This icon, an oil painting on wood, is in the Church of the Greek Patriach, St. Constantine and St. Helen in Jerusalem.

Ἡ ΒΑΪΟΦΟΡΟΣ

ὡσαννὰ τῶ ὑῶ δαβίδ. εὐλογημένος ὁ ἐρχόμενος ἐν ὀνόματι
κυρίου. ὡσαννὰ ὁ ἐν τοῖς ὑψίστοις

My doctrine is not mine, but his that sent me.

JESUS IN THE TEMPLE

Now about the midst of the feast Jesus went up into the temple and taught. And the Jews marvelled saying, How knoweth this man letters, having never learned? Jesus answered them, and said, My doctrine is not mine, but his that sent me. If any man will do his will, he shall know of the doctrine, whether it be of God, or whether I speak of myself. He that speaketh of himself seeketh his own glory: but he that seeketh his glory that sent him, the same is true, and no unrighteousness is in him.

John 7:14-18

Then cried Jesus in the temple as he taught, saying, Ye both know me, and ye know whence I am: and I am not come of myself, but he that sent me is true, whom ye know not. But I know him: for I am from him, and he hath sent me. Then they sought to take him: but no man laid hands on him, because his hour was not yet come. And many of the people believed on him, and said, When Christ cometh, will he do more miracles than these which this man hath done?

John 7:28-31

And Jesus entered into Jerusalem, and into the temple: and when he had looked round about upon all things, and now the eventide was come, he went out unto Bethany with the twelve.

Mark 11:11

Jesus Preaching in the Temple of Jerusalem. An icon from the Greek Holy of Holies in the Greek Basilica of the Nativity in Bethlehem. It is an oil painting on wood, donated to the church in 1848.

The stairway leading from Mount Zion down to The Pool of Siloam. Jesus and His disciples probably used these steps when they went to the Mount of Olives. Jesus was probably also led along this way to the hearing at the house of the High Priest. This is one of the few places in Jerusalem where a pilgrim can be certain of following the steps of Jesus.

THE PLOT

After two days was the feast of the passover, and of unleavened bread: and the chief priests and the scribes sought how they might take him by craft, and put him to death. But they said, Not on the feast day, lest there be an uproar of the people. *Mark 14; 1-2*

Then one of the twelve, called Judas Iscariot, went unto the chief priests, and said unto them, What will ye give me, and I will deliver him unto you? And they covenanted with him for thirty pieces of silver. And from that time he sought opportunity to betray him. *Matt. 26:14-16*

Ancient foundations on the Eastern slope of Mount Zion that are shown today as parts of the place of Caiaphas. In the background are the valley of Kidron, the village of Siloah, the Mount of Offense and a part of the desert of Judea.

And he will shew you a large upper room furnished and prepared: there make ready for us.

PREPARATION FOR THE SUPPER

And the first day of unleavened bread, when they killed the passover, his disciples said unto him, Where wilt thou that we go and prepare that thou mayest eat the passover? And he sendeth forth two of his disciples, and saith unto them, Go ye into the city, and there shall meet you a man bearing a pitcher of water: follow him. And wheresoever he shall go in, say ye to the goodman of the house, The Master saith, Where is the guest chamber, where I shall eat the passover with my disciples? And he will shew you a large upper room furnished and prepared: there make ready for us. And his disciples went forth, and came into the city, and they found as he had said unto them: and they made ready the passover.   *Mark 14:12-16*

The Upper Room (Coenaculum) on Mount Zion. It is built on the spot where, according to reliable ancient traditions, the last supper took place and where the disciples gathered after Jesus' departure. The first Christian Church building ever erected was located on this site, and only by accident was it not destroyed by Titus in 70 A.D. when he destroyed the Temple. In the fourth century this church was replaced by a Basilica with five naves. The Crusaders found this basilica, "Hagia Zion," destroyed. They rebuilt it, and the room we see today is part of their church. The Gothic arches were added later. The Moslems used this church as a mosque and the structures on the lefthand side and in the left corner belong to the mosque.

THE LAST SUPPER

And in the evening he cometh with the twelve. And as they sat and did eat, Jesus said, Verily I say unto you, One of you which eateth with me shall betray me. And they began to be sorrowful, and to say unto him one by one, Is it I? and another said, Is it I? And he answered and said unto them, It is one of the twelve, that dippeth with me in the dish. The Son of man indeed goeth, as it is written of him: but woe to that man by whom the Son of man is betrayed: good were it for that man if he had never been born.

And as they did eat, Jesus took bread and blessed and brake it and gave to them, and said, Take, eat: this is my body. And he took the cup, and when he had given thanks, he gave it to them: and they all drank of it. And he said unto them, This is my blood of the new testament, which is shed for many. Verily I say unto you, I will drink no more of the fruit of the vine, until that day that I drink it new in the kingdom of God.

Mark 14:17-25

The Last Supper, or the "Mystical Meal," as the Greek inscription at the top indicates. The Greek letters, omicron, omega and nu, that are written on the cross inside the halo around the head of Christ mean, "The Being," or "I Am That I Am," which is a synonym for the Hebrew "Yahweh" the name of God. The letters iota-sigma and chi-sigma are abbreviations for Jesus Christ in Greek. Above the head of St. John the Disciple is his name in Greek.

This is a section of an oil painting dated 1808 that is placed above the preparation table in the Holy of Holies in the Greek chapel of the Church of the Nativity in Bethlehem.

The Last Supper or the "Mystical Meal." The three works on this page show Jesus with the twelve disciples. The upper picture is from the cross-shaped nave of the Church of the Nativity in Bethlehem. St. John is usually shown at the right of Jesus, but in the lower left picture he is shown sitting to the left of Jesus (at Jesus' right hand). This picture is on the front of the offering box of the Ethiopian Church in Mea-Shearim. The picture at lower right is an icon in the Holy of Holies of the Greek Chapel in the Church of the Nativity in Bethlehem. It is oil on wood and was donated to the church in 1843.

The picture on the next page is oil on wood, an icon in a small Coptic chapel, the Chapel of Santa Maria in Bethlehem.

If I then, your Lord and Master, have washed your feet; ye also ought to wash one another's feet. For I have given you an example, that ye should do as I have done to you.

THE FOOTWASHING

Now before the feast of the passover, when Jesus knew that his hour was come that he should depart out of this world unto the Father, having loved his own which were in the world, he loved them unto the end. And supper being ended, the devil having now put into the heart of Judas Iscariot, Simon's son, to betray him; Jesus knowing that the Father had given all things into his hands, and that he was come from God, and went to God; He riseth from Supper, and laid aside his garments; and took a towel, and girded himself. After that he poureth water into a basin, and began to wash the deciples' feet, and to wipe them with the towel wherewith he was girded.

Then cometh he to Simon Peter: and Peter saith unto him, Lord dost thou wash my feet? Jesus answered and said unto him, What I do thou knowest not now; but thou shalt know hereafter. Peter saith unto him, Thou shalt never wash my feet. Jesus answered him, If I wash thee not, thou hast no part with me. Simon Peter saith unto him Lord not my feet only, but also my hands and my head. Jesus saith to him, He that is washed needeth not save to wash his feet, but is clean every whit: and ye are clean, but not all. For he knew who should betray him; therefore said he, Ye are not all clean.

So after he had washed their feet and had taken his garments, and was set down again, he said unto them, Know ye what I have done to you? Ye call me Master and Lord: and ye say well; for so I am. If I then, your Lord and Master, have washed your feet; ye also ought to wash one another's feet. For I have given you an example, that ye should do as I have done to you.   *John 13:1-15*

The Last Supper and the Footwashing. An icon painted on wood in the Saint Constantine and St. Helena Monastery Church, of the Greek Orthodox Patriarchate, which is located above the Church of the Holy Sepulchre in Jerusalem. The Greek inscription on the upper picture reads *"ho mystikos deipnos"*--the "mystical meal," which is the Greek name for the Last Supper. The Greek inscription on the top of the lower picture reads *"ho hieros nipter"*--the "Holy Basin," to commemorate the footwashing.

Ο ΜΥΣΤΙΚΟΣ ΔΕΙΠΝΟΣ

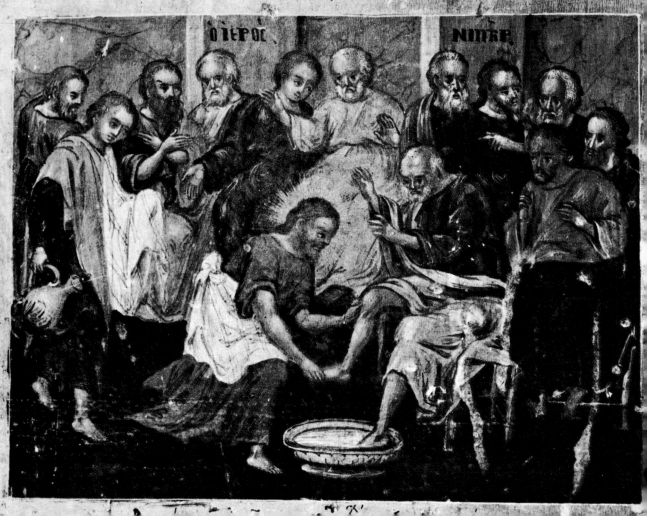

Ο ΙΕΡΟΣ ΝΙΠΤΗΡ

Mount of Olives with the Basilica of the Nations, in the Garden of Gethsemane. The Church is run by the Franciscan Fathers (Terra Santa). Above the Church of the Nations is the Russian Convent and the Magdalene Church.

GETHSEMANE

And when they had sung an hymn, they went out into the mount of Olives. And Jesus saith unto them, All ye shall be offended because of me this night: for it is written, I will smite the shepherd, and the sheep shall be scattered. But after that I am risen, I will go before you into Galilee. But Peter said unto him, Although all shall be offended, yet will not I. And Jesus saith unto him, Verily I say unto thee, That this day, even in this night, before the cock crow twice, thou shalt deny me thrice. But he spake the more vehemently, If I should die with thee, I will not deny thee in any wise. Likewise also said they all.

Mark 14:26-31

An olive tree in the Garden of Gethsemane, one of the seven oldest trees in the garden. These trees are many hundreds of years old and could doubtless be offshoots of those olive trees that stood here in the time of Christ. The stones from the olives of these trees are used by the custodian of the Holy Land as gift rosaries for the pilgrims.

GETHSEMANE PRAYER

And when he was at the place, he said unto them, Pray that ye enter not into temptation. And he was withdrawn from them about a stone cast, and kneeled down and prayed, saying, Father, if thou be willing, remove this cup from me: nevertheless not my will, but thine, be done. And there appeared an angel unto him from heaven, strengthening him. And being in an agony he prayed more earnestly: and his sweat was as it were great drops of blood falling down to the ground.
And when he rose up from prayer and was coming to his disciples, he found them sleeping for sorrow, And said unto them, Why sleep ye? rise and pray, lest ye enter into temptation.   *Luke 22:40-46*

And he taketh with him Peter and James and John, and began to be sore amazed, and to be very heavy; and saith unto them, My soul is exceeding sorrowful unto death: tarry ye here, and watch. And he went forward a little, and fell on the ground, and prayed that, if it were possible, the hour might pass from him.   *Mark 14:33-35*

And he cometh, and findeth them sleeping, and saith unto Peter, Simon, sleepest thou? couldest not thou watch one hour? Watch ye and pray, lest ye enter into temptation. The spirit truly is ready, but the flesh is weak. And again he sent away and prayed, and spake the same words. And when he returned, he found them asleep again, (for their eyes were heavy,) neither wist they what to answer him. And he cometh the third time, and saith unto them, Sleep on now, and take your rest: it is enough, the hour is come: behold, the Son of man is betrayed into the hands of sinners. Rise, let us go; lo, he that betrayeth me is at hand.
     Matt. 26:40-46

Father, if Thou be willing, remove this cup from me: nevertheless not my will, but thine, be done. And there appeared an angel unto him from heaven, strengthening him.

The Prayer of the Lord (as the Greek inscription in the picture, *"he proseuche tou Kuriou"* says). An icon on the altar wall of the Greek Golgotha Chapel in the Church of the Holy Sepulchre. This picture is part of the total depiction of the Passion of Christ. It was painted about a hundred years ago by a Greek monk. All the icons are covered with silver reliefs and placed in heavy brass frames. Originally only the hands, feet and faces were seen through the silver covers.

Ἡ ΠΡΟΣΕΥΧΗ ΤΟΥ ΚΥΡΙΟΥ

Jesus receiving a cup from an angel. In the upper right corner, God the Father is watching the prayer scene. This is a marble relief in the Basilica of the Garden of Gethsemane (the Church of the Nations).

The Grotto of Betrayal and Imprisonment. This Grotto has been the property of the Franciscan order since 1392. It is near the tomb of Mary, very near the Garden of Gethsemane. This probably was the place where the oil press of the old farm, Gethsemane, stood. (Gethsemane means "oil press" in Hebrew.)

The Golden Gate in the East Wall of the Temple yard, built in the fifth century on the same location where the Zusan Gate of Herod previously stood. According to tradition, Jesus entered Jerusalem through the Zusan Gate. The Jews expect the arrival of the Messiah through this gate, and the Moslems believe that the last judgment by Mohammed will take place here.

Left: Entry into Jerusalem. An icon in the Holy of Holies in the Greek Chapel of the Church of the Nativity in Bethlehem. Oil on wood. This icon was donated to the church in 1848. The Greek inscription at the top of the picture reads, *"Ton Baion,"* or *"Of the Palm Branches,"* to commemorate Palm Sunday.

Friend, wherefore art thou come?

THE BETRAYAL

And while he yet spake, lo, Judas, one of the twelve, came, and with him a great multitude with swords and staves, from the chief priests and elders of the people. Now he that betrayed him gave them a sign, saying, Whomsoever I shall kiss, that same is he: hold him fast. And forthwith he came to Jesus, and said, Hail, master; and kissed him. And Jesus said unto him, Friend, wherefore art thou come? Then came they and laid hands on Jesus and took him.

And, behold, one of them which were with Jesus stretched out his hand, and drew his sword, and struck a servant of the high priest's, and smote off his ear. Then said Jesus unto him, Put up again thy sword into his place: for all they that take the sword shall perish with the sword. Thinkest thou that I cannot now pray to my Father, and he shall presently give me more than twelve legions of angels? But how then shall the scriptures be fulfilled, that thus it must be?

In that same hour said Jesus to the multitudes, Are ye come out as against a thief with swords and staves for to take me? I sat daily with you teaching in the temple, and ye laid no hold on me. But all this was done, that the scriptures of the prophets might be fulfilled. Then all the disciples forsook him, and fled.   *Matt. 26:47-56*

The Kiss of Judas. A Mosaic in the Basilica of Gethsemane done by Barberis in 1924.

DIXIT IESVS AMICE AD QVID VENISTI? MATTH XXVI·50
IVDA OSCVLO FILIVM HOMINIS TRADIS? LVC XXII·4

Right: The Interior of the Basilica in the Garden of Gethsemane. The present church was built in the years 1919-1924. The project was undertaken by the Franciscan Fathers and was constructed by Barluzzi. Already, in the fourth, eighth, and twelfth centuries there had been churches on this spot, which were destroyed from time to time. The altar stands behind a bare rock on which Jesus might have prayed. The mosaic, which was done by Barberis, depicts Jesus after he was forsaken.

A view from the Citadel of the old city of Jerusalem, looking toward the Mount of Olives at right.

JESUS BEFORE THE HIGH PRIEST

Then the band and the captain and officers of the Jews took Jesus, and bound him, and led him away to Annas first; for he was father in law to Caiaphas, which was the high priest that same year. Now Caiaphas was he, which gave counsel to the Jews, that it was expedient that one man should die for the people.

And Simon Peter followed Jesus, and so did another disciple: that disciple was known unto the high priest, and went in with Jesus into the palace of the high priest. But Peter stood at the door without. Then went out that other disciple, which was known unto the high priest, and spake unto her that kept the door, and brought in Peter. Then saith the damsel that kept the door unto Peter, Art not thou also one of this man's disciples? He saith, I am not. And the servants and officers stood there, who had made a fire of coals; for it was cold: and they warmed themselves: and Peter stood with them, and warmed himself. The high priest then asked Jesus of his disciples, and of his doctrine. Jesus answered him, I spake openly to the world; I ever taught in the synagogue, and in the temple, whither the Jews always resort; and in secret have I said nothing. Why askest thou me? ask them which heard me, what I have said unto them: behold, they know what I said. And when he had thus spoken, one of the officers which stood by struck Jesus with the palm of his hand, saying, Answerest thou the high priest so? Jesus answered him, If I have spoken evil, bear witness of the evil: but if well, why smitest thou me? Now Annas had sent him bound unto Caiaphas the high priest. *John 18:12-24*

The American Chapel of the Holy Angels. The American tradition locates the Palace of Annas here, and specifies it as the cell in which Christ was imprisoned.

Jesus Before the High Priest, Annas, as the Greek inscription in the picture indicates. This is an icon on the altar wall of the Greek Golgotha Chapel in the Church of the Holy Sepulchre.

*Art not thou also one of his
disciples?*

PETER'S DENIAL

And Simon Peter stood and warmed himself. They
said therefore unto him, Art not thou also one
of his disciples? He denied it, and said, I am not.
One of the servants of the high priest, being his
kinsman whose ear Peter cut off, saith, Did not I
see thee in the garden with him? Peter then denied
again: and immediately the cock crew.

John 18:25-27

The Prison in which Christ was
kept, under what is now the church
of St. Peter, in Gallicantu, in the
so-called Palace of Caiaphas.

Now Peter sat without in the palace: and a damsel
came unto him, saying, Thou also wast with Jesus
of Galilee. But he denied before them all saying,
I know not what thou sayest. And when he was
gone out into the porch, another maid saw him,
and said unto them that were there, This fellow
was also with Jesus of Nazareth. And again he
denied with an oath, I do not know the man. And
after a while came unto him they that stood by,
and said to Peter, Surely thou also art one of them;
for thy speech betrayeth thee. Then began he to
curse and to swear, saying, I know not the man.
And immediately the cock crew. And Peter remembered the word of Jesus, which said unto him,
Before the cock crow, thou shalt deny me thrice.
And he went out, and wept bitterly.

Matt. 26:69-75

The Church of St. Peter in Gallicantu (where St. Peter stood when
the cock crew), near the eastern
slope of Mount Zion. It is dedicated to the commemoration of
the sorrow of St. Peter. The
church belongs to the Monastery
of the Assumptionist Fathers, who
built it in 1931 upon the ruins
of the Byzantine church. In the
background, at left, can be seen
the Temple, with the Dome of
the Rock and the El-Aksa Mosque.
On the right is the village Silwan
(Siloah), and the Mount of Olives.

Then said they all, Art thou
then the Son of God? And
he said unto them, Ye say
that I am.

JESUS BEFORE CAIAPHAS

Now the chief priests, and elders, and all the council, sought false witness against Jesus, to put him to death; but found none: yea, though many false witnesses came, yet found they none. At the last came two false witnesses, and said, This fellow said, I am able to destroy the temple of God, and to build it in three days.

Matt. 26:59-61

And as soon as it was day, the elders of the people and the chief priests and the scribes came together, and led him into their council, saying, Art thou the Christ? tell us. And he said unto them, If I tell you, ye will not believe: And if I also ask you, ye will not answer me, nor let me go. Hereafter shall the Son of man sit on the right hand of the power of God. Then said they all, Art thou then the Son of God? And he said unto them, Ye say that I am. And they said, What need we any further witness? for we ourselves have heard of his own mouth.

Luke 22:66-71

Jesus before Caiaphas. A section of an icon on the altar wall of the Greek Golgotha Chapel in the Holy Sepulchre Church. The Greek title inscription reads *"he pros Kaiapha,"* meaning "Before Caiaphas." The Greek letters *omicron, omega* and *nu* on the halo represent a symbolic name of God, "I Am that I Am," or "The Being."

Η ΠΡΟΣ ΚΑΪΑΦΑ

THE DEATH OF JUDAS

Then Judas, which had betrayed him, when he saw that he was condemned, repented himself, and brought again the thirty pieces of silver to the chief priests and elders, Saying, I have sinned in that I have betrayed the innocent blood. And they said, What is that to us? see thou to that. And he cast down the pieces of silver in the temple, and departed, and went and hanged himself. And the chief priests took the silver pieces, and said, It is not lawful for to put them into the treasury, because it is the price of blood. And they took counsel, and bought with them the potter's field, to bury strangers in. Wherefore that field was called, The field of blood, unto this day.

Matt. 27:3-8

And in those days Peter stood up in the midst of the disciples, and said, (the number of names together were about an hundred and twenty,) Men and bretheren, this scripture must needs have been fulfilled, which the Holy Ghost by the mouth of David spake before concerning Judas, which was guide to them that took Jesus. For he was numbered with us, and had obtained part of this ministry. Now this man purchased a field with the reward of iniquity; and falling headlong, he burst asunder in the midst, and all his bowels gushed out. And it was known unto all the dwellers at Jerusalem; insomuch as that field is called in their proper tongue, Aceldama, that is to say, The field of blood.

Acts 1:15-19

Jewish graveyard from the time of Jesus, located in the lower Hinnom Valley. According to perpetuating ancient tradition, this place is supposed to be the "Potter's Field" that became known as the "Field of Blood" (Hekeldama) after it was bought by the priests with the thirty pieces of silver which Judas had left in the Temple.

68

70

The medieval "Hakeldama". Monastic cells dating from the sixth century are here. The arch was built by the crusaders. Here the knights of St. John buried the pilgrims who died in their hospices (hotel).

Left, Top: A natural cave with tombs chiselled into it. In the medieval period it was enlarged by a stone wall. The hole in the ceiling is an artificial pit through which the corpses were let down into the vault.

Left, Bottom: An entrance into the tomb system that expands deep into the rock. The burial pits, corridors and doors are chiselled out of the natural stone.

71

THE TRIAL OF JESUS

And straightway in the morning the chief priests
held a consultation with the elders and scribes
and the whole council, and bound Jesus, and carried
him away, and delivered him to Pilate.

Mark 15:1

Then led they Jesus from Caiaphas unto the hall
of judgment: and it was early; and they themselves went not into the judgment hall, lest they
should be defiled; but that they might eat the passover. Pilate then went out unto them, and said,
What accusation bring ye against this man? They
answered and said unto him, If he were not a male-
factor, we would not have delivered him up unto
thee. Then said Pilate unto them, Take ye him,
and judge him according to your law. The Jews
therefore said unto him, It is not lawful for us
to put any man to death. That the saying of Jesus
might be fulfilled, which he spake, signifying what
death he should die.

John 18:28-32

The Ecce Homo Basilica of the
Sisters of Zion. This convent was
built in the years of 1857-1862.
The ancient gate is part of a three-
arch gate that was built in 135 A.D.
by Hadrian. It was the Eastern
Gate of Aelia Capitolina(the Roman
name given to Jerusalem after the
destruction of the Temple in 70
A.D.) The central part of the
arch spans the nearby Via Dolorosa
Since the sixteenth century this
gate has been mistakenly identified
as the "Ecce Homo" Gate (Behold
the Man) of Pilate.

A model of the Fort of Antonia
as it was reconstructed (only partially accurately) by the Sisters of
Zion. The Fort of Antonia was
erected in the years 37-35 B.C.
by Herod the Great and was named
in honor of the ruling Roman
Triumvir, Mark Antony. According
to a medieval Jerusalem tradition,
this is supposed to be the place
where Jesus was sentenced by Pilate.

73

The Last Supper. A ceramic tile in the Etchmiadzin Chapel in the Church of the Armenian Patriarch, St. James.

Left: The citadel near the Jaffa gate at the westernmost part of the old city of Jerusalem. The fortress kept its appearance during the time of the Mamelukes and the Turks. Underneath the Minarette, called David's Tower, are the foundations of Phasael Tower, one of the towers with which Herod the Great fortified his palace in 24 B.C. The Roman procurators stopped at this palace when they came from their residences in Caesarea to Jerusalem. This place is probably the site of the Praetorium, where the trial of Jesus was held.

JESUS BEFORE PILATE

And they began to accuse him, saying, We found this fellow perverting the nation, and forbidding to give tribute to Caesar, saying that he himself is Christ a King. And Pilate asked him, saying, Art thou the King of the Jews? And he answered him and said, Thou sayest it. Then said Pilate to the chief priests and to the people, I find no fault in this man. And they were the more fierce, saying, He stirreth up the people, teaching throughout all Jewry, beginning from Galilee to this place.

Luke 23:2-5

Jesus before Pilate. A section from the ceiling painting of the Greek Golgotha Chapel in the Holy Sepulchre Church. Oil on heavy linen.

Then Pilate entered into the judgment hall again and called Jesus, and said unto him, Art thou the King of the Jews? Jesus answered him, Sayest thou this thing of thyself, or did others tell it thee of me? Pilate answered, Am I a Jew? Thine own nation and the chief priests have delivered thee unto me: what hast thou done? Jesus answered, My kingdom is not of this world: if my kingdom were of this world, then would my servants fight, that I should not be delivered to the Jews: but now is my kingdom not from hence. Pilate therefore said unto him, Art thou a king then? Jesus answered, Thou sayest that I am a king. To this end was I born, and for this cause came I into the world, that I should bear witness unto the truth. Every one that is of the truth heareth my voice. Pilate saith unto him, What is truth?

John 18:33-38

Jesus before Pilate. A section of an icon on the altar wall of the same chapel.

The Coronation with the Crown of Thorns. Detail from the ceiling painting in the Greek Golgotha Chapel of the Church of the Holy Sepulchre. The Greek inscription reads, "And they stripped him, and put on him a scarlet robe. And when they had plaited a crown of thorns, they put it upon his head."

The torturing of Jesus. A ceramic tile in the Etchmiadzin Chapel in St. James Church, the Church of the Armenian Patriarchate. The tile was brought from Qutahia (Armenia) in the seventeenth century.

I find in him no fault at all.

RELEASE OF A PRISONER
AT THE PASSOVER

And when he had said this, he went out again unto the Jews, and saith unto them, I find in him no fault at all. But ye have a custom, that I should release unto you one at the passover: will ye therefore that I release unto you the King of the Jews? Then cried they all again, saying, Not this man, but Barabbas. Now Barabbas was a robber.

John 18:38-40

Now at that feast he released unto them one prisoner, whomsoever they desired. And there was one named Barabbas, which lay bound with them that had made insurrection with him, who had committed murder in the insurrection. And the multitude crying aloud began to desire him to do as he had ever done unto them. But Pilate answered them saying, Will ye that I release unto you the King of the Jews? For he knew that the chief priests had delivered him for envy. But the chief priests moved the people, that he should rather release Barabbas unto them. And Pilate answered and said again unto them, What will ye then that I shall do with him whom ye call the King of the Jews? And they cried out again, Crucify him.

Mark 15:6-13

Christ Imprisoned. An oil painting in the Church of the Nativity in Bethlehem.

The prison in which Christ was held, shown in the Orthodox Praetorium on the Via Dolorosa. The room itself is an old rock tomb that was recently reconstructed by the Greek Monks as a prison. For the reconstruction they used old paintings like the picture on the left.

The old rock tombs that are shown today by the Greek Monks as the prison where Christ was held. They also show the prison in the upper left picture as the one in which Barabbas was imprisoned.

The Via Dolorosa with the "Ecce Homo" arch. At the right is the Chapel of Condemnation built in 1903 in Byzantine style. It belongs to the Bible Institute of the Franciscan order, located here since 1927. It has a very interesting archaeological collection and an important library.

Right: The Mount of Olives, with the Garden of Gethsemane and the Basilica of the Nations as seen from the Temple yard above.

And when Herod saw Jesus, he was exceedingly glad: for he was desirous to see him of a long season, because he had heard many things of him, and he hoped to have seen some miracle done by him. Then he questioned with him in many words, but he answered him nothing.

JESUS BEFORE HEROD

When Pilate heard of Galilee he asked whether the man were a Galilaean. And as soon as he knew that he belonged unto Herod's jurisdiction, he sent him to Herod, who himself also was at Jerusalem at that time. And when Herod saw Jesus, he was exceeding glad: for he was desirous to see him of a long season, because he had heard many things of him; and he hoped to have seen some miracle done by him. Then he questioned with him in many words; but he answered him nothing. And the chief priests and scribes stood and vehemently accused him. And Herod with his men of war set him at naught, and mocked him, and arrayed him in a gorgeous robe, and sent him again to Pilate. And the same day Pilate and Herod were made friends together: for before they were at enmity between themselves. And Pilate, when he had called together the people, Said unto them, Ye have brought this man unto me, as one that perverteth the people: and, behold, I, having examined him before you, have found no fault in this man touching those things whereof ye accuse him: No, nor yet Herod: for I sent you to him; and lo, nothing worthy of death is done unto him. I will therefore chastise him, and release him.

Luke 23:6-16

A bird's-eye-view of the Jewish Quarter of the old city of Jerusalem, photographed in the summer of 1967. In the time of Jesus this was the area where the Palace of the Hasmonean kings was located and it is here that Herod Antipas stayed whenever he was in Jerusalem.

Left: The lower part of the torture column as shown in the Chapel of Mocking, in the aisle of the Holy Sepulchre Church.

Bottom left: The torture column at the entrance of the Coptic Patriarchate Church, above the Holy Sepulchre Church. This is traditionally the Ninth Station of the Cross.

Bottom right: The lower part of the torture column, made of porphyry which stands on a side altar in the Chapel of Appearance in the Latin (Catholic) part of the Church of the Holy Sepulchre.

Jesus before Pilate, as the Greek inscription indicates. Seen here also, in the halo around the head of
Christ near the three Greek letters representing the name of God. These icons are from the altar wall
of the Greek Golgotha Chapel in the Holy Sepulchre Church.

Pilate therefore went forth again, and saith unto them, Behold, I bring him forth to you, that ye may know that I find no fault in him.

TORTURING OF JESUS

Then Pilate therefore took Jesus, and scourged him. And the soldiers platted a crown of thorns, and put it on his head, and they put on him a purple robe, And said, Hail, King of the Jews: and they smote him with their hands. Pilate therefore went forth again, and saith unto them, Behold, I bring him forth to you, that ye may know that I find no fault in him. *John 19:1-4*

And they stripped him, and put on him a scarlet robe. And when they had platted a crown of thorns they put it upon his head, and a reed in his right hand: and they bowed the knee before him, and mocked him, saying, Hail, King of the Jews! And they spit upon him, and took the reed, and smote him on the head. And after that they had mocked him, they took the robe off from him, and put his own raiment on him.

Matt. 27:28-31

The torturing of Jesus. A section of an icon on the altar wall of the Greek Golgotha Chapel in the Church of the Holy Sepulchre.

THE SHOUT TO CRUCIFY

Then came Jesus forth, wearing the crown of thorns, and the purple robe. And Pilate saith unto them, Behold the man! When the chief priests therefore and officers saw him, they cried out, saying, Crucify him, crucify him. Pilate saith unto them, Take ye him; for I find no fault in him. The Jews answered him, We have a law, and by our law he ought to die, because he made himself the Son of God.

John 19:5-7

"Ecce Homo" (Behold the man). An oil painting in a chapel of the Armenian monastery near the Basilica of the Nativity in Bethlehem.

JESUS OR CAESAR

When Pilate therefore heard that saying, he was the more afraid; and went again into the judgment hall, and saith unto Jesus, Whence are thou? But Jesus gave him no answer. Then saith Pilate unto him, Speakest thou not unto me? knowest thou not that I have power to crucify thee, and have power to release thee? Jesus answered, Thou couldest have no power at all against me, except it were given thee from above: therefore he that delivered me unto thee hath the greater sin. And from thenceforth Pilate sought to release him: but the Jews cried out, saying, If thou let this man go, thou art not Caesar's friend: whosoever maketh himself a king speaketh against Caesar. When Pilate therefore heard that saying, he brought Jesus forth, and sat down in the judgment seat in a place that is called the Pavement, but in the Hebrew, Gabbatha. And it was the preparation of the passover, and about the sixth hour: and he saith unto the Jews, Behold your King: But they cried out, away with him, crucify him. Pilate saith unto them, Shall I crucify your King? The chief priests answered, We have no king but Caesar.

John 19:8-15

Right
This picture shows the grooves that were made on the Lithostrotos so that the horses coming into the court would not slip.

The Lithostrotos (the stone path). The Roman street pavement was excavated by the Sisters of Zion. It continues under the Via Dolorosa and under the nearby building of the Chapel of the Condemnation, down to the Orthodox Praetorium. Although it cannot be archaelogically proved, it may be the original pavement of the fort of Antonia. If this is the praetorium of the Roman governor of Jerusalem, this would be the place where Jesus was sentenced.

I am innocent of the blood
of this just person: see ye
to it.

PILATE WASHING HIS HANDS

When he was set down on the judgment seat, his
wife sent unto him, saying, Have thou nothing
to do with that just man: for I have suffered many
things this day in a dream because of him. But the
chief priests and elders persuaded the multitude
that they should ask Barabbas, and destroy Jesus.
The governor answered and said unto them, Whether
of the twain will ye that I release unto you? They
said, Barabbas. Pilate saith unto them, What shall
I do then with Jesus which is called Christ? They
all say unto him, Let him be crucified. And the
governor said, Why, what evil hath he done? But
they cried out the more, saying, Let him be crucified. When Pilate saw that he could prevail nothing,
but that rather a tumult was made, he took water,
and washed his hands before the multitude, saying,
I am innocent of the blood of this just person: see
ye to it. Then answered all the people, and said,
His blood be on us, and on our children.

Matt. 27:24-25

Pilate washes his hands as a sign
of innocence in the crucifixion
of Jesus. A section from the
ceiling painting in the Greek Golgotha Chapel in the Church of
the Holy Sepulchre.

And there followed him a great company of people, and of women, which also bewailed and lamented him.

ON THE WAY TO THE CROSS

And as they led him away, they laid hold upon one Simon, a Cyrenian, coming out of the country, and on him they laid the cross, that he might bear it after Jesus.   And there followed him a great company of people, and of women, which also bewailed and lamented him.   But Jesus turning unto them said, Daughters of Jerusalem, weep not for me, but weep for yourselves, and for your children.   *Luke 23:26-28*

And they compel one Simon a Cyrenian, who passed by, coming out of the country, the father of Alexander and Rufus, to bear his cross.

Mark 15:21

A procession of pilgrims on the Via Dolorosa. Every Friday there is a procession of the Franciscans going through all the stations of the Via Dolorosa to commemorate the day on which Jesus was crucified.

Left: The Third Station of the Cross. This Chapel was built in 1947 by the Polish Community in Jerusalem. The sculpture is by C. Zieliensky.

Franciscan Monks praying in the Greek Golgotha Chapel.

ΑΙΡΕΙ ΤΟΝ ΣΤΑΥΡΟΝ

Simon of Cyrene helping Jesus carry the cross. The Greek inscription says, "He takes up the cross." The inscription on the scroll in the hand of the Roman soldier "INRI" stands for "*Iesus Nazerenus Rex Iudaiorum*" which means Jesus of Nazareth, King of the Jews.

Right: Veronica handing a handkerchief to Jesus, a relief from the nineteenth century, located in the entrance of the Church of St. Veronica.

The Greek Golgotha Chapel with the altar of the crucifixion. The altar is built on the top of the sixteen-foot high rock on the top of the hill of Golgotha. Parts of the rock can be seen. The entire Golgotha Road is inside the church of the Holy Sepulchre.

Left: The Chapel of St. Veronica on the Via Dolorosa, the Sixth Station of the Cross. This chapel was restored recently and is maintained by the Little Sisters of Jesus, a Convent of the Greek Catholic Church. Pope Paul VI stopped here for prayer during his visit to the Holy Land in 1964.

The Hadrian Arch at the entrance of the Roman Forums, from the second century. The Forum was destroyed by Emperor Constantine when he made his excavations, looking for relics. This Arch is inside the Alexander Hostel.

Parts of the City Wall and the City Gate, that are today inside the Russian Alexander Hostel, near the Holy Sepulchre. Inside the glass box in front of the altar is the old threshold of the gate upon which Jesus probably stepped, carrying the cross, when He left the city through this gate, toward Golgotha.

The Face of Jesus on Veronica's Handkerchief. *Vere icon* signifies "the true image." Since the name of the legendary woman who gave Jesus her handkerchief so that he could wipe his sweat was not known, and since the true face of Jesus remained on this handkerchief, the name Veronica, from *"vere icon"* was given to her. This picture is an oil painting from the eighteenth century and is hung above the altar of the Veronica Chapel.

Byzantine arches near the Veronica Chapel, probably remainders of the Monaste of Holy Kosmas and Damian from the sixth century.

The Church of the Holy Sepulchre in Jerusalem. It was built above the site where the place of Golgotha and the tomb of Jesus were located in the fourth century. In 326-335 the first church was built here by Emperor Constantine. During the succeeding years the church was destroyed and reconstructed many times. The rebuilders were Modestos (629), Constantine Monomachos (1048) and the Crusaders (1149). Since 1961 the building has been totally renovated.

CRUCIFIXION

And they bring him unto the place Golgotha, which is, being interpreted, the place of a skull. And they gave him to drink wine mingled with myrrh; but he received it not. And they crucified him.   *Mark 15:22-24*

And when they were come to the place, which is called Calvary, there they crucified him, and the malefactors, one on the right hand, and the other on the left. Then said Jesus, Father, forgive them; for they know not what they do.
                    Luke 23:33-34a

Gordon's Golgotha. When General Gordon discovered the garden tomb in 1882 he believed that this hill, north of the Damascus Gate, was the hill of Golgotha. He believed that the hill had the shape of a skull (Golgotha, in Aramaic, means the skull). At present there is a Moslem cemetery on this hill.

CASTING LOTS OVER THE GARMENT

And when they had crucified him they parted his garments, casting lots upon them, what every man should take. And it was the third hour, and they crucified him. And the superscription of his accusation was written over, THE KING OF THE JEWS. And with him they crucify two thieves; the one on his right hand, and the other on his left. And the scripture was fulfilled, which saith, And he was numbered with the transgressors. And they that passed by railed on him, wagging their heads, and saying, Ah, thou that destroyest the temple, and buildest it in three days. Save thyself, and come down from the cross. Likewise also the chief priests mocking said among themselves with the scribes, He saved others; himself he cannot save. Let Christ the King of Israel descend now from the cross, that we may see and believe.

Mark 15:24-32

This title then read many of the Jews: for the place where Jesus was crucified was nigh to the city: and it was written in Hebrew, and Greek, and Latin. Then said the chief priests of the Jews to Pilate, Write not, The King of the Jews; but that he said, I am King of the Jews. Pilate answered, What I have written I have written.

John 19:20-22

Gambling over the clothes of Jesus. A section from the ceiling painting in the Greek Golgotha Chapel in the Church of the Holy Sepulchre.

A Bird's-eye view of the Old City of Jerusalem. In the foreground are the Holy Sepulchre and the German Lutheran Church of the Savior. In the background is the Haram Eshsharif (the temple court), with the Dome of the Rock and the Valley of Kedron. The numbers represent the traditional Stations of the Cross: 1) where Jesus was condemned; 2) where Jesus lifted the cross upon His shoulder; 3) where Jesus fell under the cross; 4) where Jesus met His mother; 5) where Simon of Cyrene helped Jesus carry the cross; 6) where Veronica handed Jesus the handkerchief; 7) where Jesus fell the second time; 8) where Jesus spoke to the weeping women; 9) where Jesus fell the third time; 10) where Jesus was undressed and given the bitter drink; 11) where Jesus was nailed to the cross; 12) where Jesus died on the cross; 13) where Jesus' body was put on his mother's lap; 14) where Jesus was buried.

The Crucifixion altar in the Greek Golgotha Chapel in the Church of the Holy Sepulchre. Many of the pictures in this book can be found behind the framed silver reliefs in the background.

114

The Latin (Catholic) Golgotha Chapel with the Altar of the Nailing to the Cross. The altar table was made by the Italian artist, Portigiani, in 1588. On the left is the small altar of Our Lady of Sorrows made by a Portuguese artist in the eighteenth century. This is where Mary was supposed to have stood when her Son was crucified.

Lord, remember me when thou comest into thy Kingdom.

PRAYER OF ONE OF THE THIEVES

And one of the malefactors which were hanged railed on him, saying, If thou be Christ, save thyself and us. But the other answering rebuked him, saying, Dost not thou fear God, seeing thou art in the same condemnation? And we indeed justly; for we receive the due reward of our deeds: but this man hath done nothing amiss. And he said unto him, Verily I say unto thee, today shalt thou be with me in paradise. And it was about the sixth hour. And the sun was darkened, and the veil of the temple was rent in the midst.

Luke 23:39-45

The Crucifixion of Jesus. An icon from the altar wall of the Greek Golgotha Chapel of the Church of the Holy Sepulchre. Note the skull under the cross. This is found on many icons and is supposed to be the skull of Adam who, according to tradition, was buried just underneath the place where the cross of Jesus stood. The blood of Jesus that flows out of his wounds streams onto the head of Adam and purifies him and all human beings from the original sin. The Greek inscription says *"he staurosis tou kuriou"*, the crucifixion of the Lord. The names of the two criminals who were crucified with him are written on the crosses--Demas to the left and Kestas to the right, while the inscription, "INRI", "Jesus of Nazareth, King of the Jews," is on the cross of Christ.

117

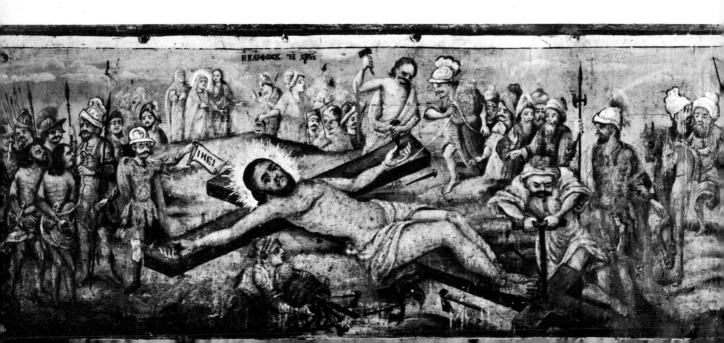

rucifixion of Jesus. The silver cover of the Book of the Gospels in St. Mark's Church of the
ites. At the four corners are the symbols of the four evangelists; the winged man for Matth
d ox for Luke; the winged lion for Mark and the eagle for John. At the bottom of the cr
ft, Mary is kneeling, and on the right are the symbols of Easter. Under the cross is the s

left: Jesus receiving myrrh with wine. A section from the ceiling painting of the Greek G
l.

m, left: Jesus being nailed to the cross. An oil painting in the altar room of the Greek G
l. The Greek inscription reads, "he karphosis tou Christou," meaning, "The Nailing of C

THE BELOVED DISCIPLE

And all his acquaintance, and the women that
followed him from Galilee, stood afar off, beholding
these things.   *Luke 23:49*

Now there stood by the cross of Jesus his mother,
and his mother's sister, Mary, the wife of Cleophas,
and Mary Magdalene.   When Jesus therefore saw
his mother, and the disciple standing by, whom
he loved, he saith unto his mother, Woman, behold
thy son!   Then saith he to the disciple, Behold
thy mother!   and from that hour that disciple
took her unto his own home.   *John 19:25-27*

The Disciple John under the Cross.
An upright, semi-plastic picture
coated with silver and jewelry, located on the crucifixion altar of
the Greek Golgotha Chapel.

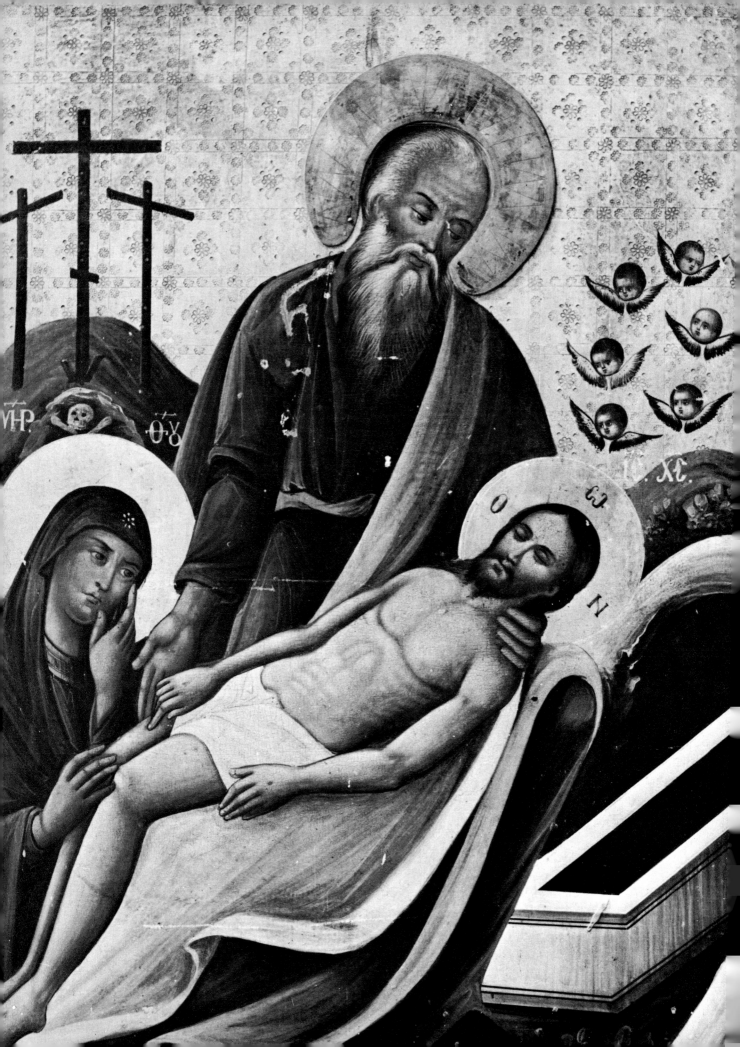

The lowering from the cross. Joseph of Arimathea and Nicodemus are lowering Jesus' body from the cross with the help of St. John. The three Marys are sitting in the lower right corner of the picture. The old Greek inscription reads "*He apokathelosis tou kuriou*," meaning, "The lowering of the Lord." It is an icon from the altar wall of the Greek Golgotha Chapel.

Left: Jesus in the arms of Joseph of Arimathea, with Mary kneeling next to them. Behind Jesus is the open coffin. The Greek inscriptions say "Mother of God" and "Jesus Christ." The icon, oil on wood, is from the Church of the Annunciation of the Greek Catholic Patriarchate Church, near the Jaffa Gate in Jerusalem.

THE LAST CRY FROM THE CROSS

And when the sixth hour was come, there was darkness over the whole land until the ninth hour. And at the ninth hour Jesus cried with a loud voice, saying, Eloi, Eloi, lama sa-bach-tha-ni? which is, being interpreted, My God, my God, why hast thou forsaken me?   *Mark 15:33-34*

After this, Jesus knowing that all things were now accomplished, that the scripture might be fulfilled, saith, I thirst. Now there was set a vessel full of vinegar: and they filled a sponge with vinegar, and put it to his mouth. When Jesus therefore had received the vinegar, he said, It is finished: and he bowed his head, and gave up the ghost.
                John 19:28-30

Jesus, when he had cried again with a loud voice, yielded up the ghost. And, behold, the veil of the temple was rent in twain from the top to the bottom; and the earth did quake, and the rocks rent; and the graves were opened; and many bodies of the saints which slept arose, and came out of the graves after his resurrection, and went into the holy city, and appeared unto many. Now when the centurion, and they that were with him, watching Jesus, saw the earthquake, and those things that were done, they feared greatly, saying, Truly this was the Son of God.   *Matt. 27:50-54*

The crucifixion of Jesus. A bronze relief in the Latin (Catholic) altar of the Golgotha Chapel. It was made by the Italian artist Portigiani in 1588, and was donated to the church by Ferdinand di Medici, the Archduke of Tuscany.

The lowering from the cross. An oil painting over the preparation table in the Greek Golgotha Chapel.

Right: The crucified Lord with Mary and John. An icon, oil on wood, in the cave of the Nativity in Bethlehem. The Greek inscription reads, "*He staurosis,*" "The Crucifixion."

The lamentation over Jesus. An oil painting in the Angel's Chapel in the Armenian Convent. Probably from the sixteenth century.

They shall look on him whom they pierced.

THE DEATH OF JESUS

The Jews therefore, because it was the preparation, that the bodies should not remain upon the cross on the sabbath day, (for that sabbath day was an high day,) besought Pilate that their legs might be broken, and that they might be taken away. Then came the soldiers, and brake the legs of the first, and of the other which was crucified with him. But when they came to Jesus, and saw that he was dead already, they brake not his legs: But one of the soldiers with a spear pierced his side, and forthwith came there out blood and water. And he that saw it bare record, and his record is true: and he knoweth that he saith true, that ye might believe. For these things were done, that the scripture should be fulfilled, A bone of him shall not be broken. And again another scripture saith, They shall look on him whom they pierced.

John 19:31-37

A Roman soldier pierces Jesus' side with his spear while other soldiers break the legs of the two crucified criminals. Only the bones of Jesus were not broken. A section from the ceiling painting in the Greek Golgotha Chapel.

Left: The Entrance to the Church of the Holy Sepulchre. The Roman facade dates from the time of the Crusaders. In the foreground there is a Greek Orthodox procession.

A view from the entrance of the Church of Holy Sepulchre toward the Rotunda and the Sepulchre. The wrought-iron candlestick on the left marks the place where the three Marys stood while Jesus' body was anointed.

The Holy Sepulchre viewed from the dome of the Church of the Holy Sepulchre. Burned down in 1810, it was rebuilt in Greek Rococo style. The church was nearly destroyed again in the great earthquake of 1927. The bishops of the various denominations could not agree on the terms for restoring the church, and the British Mandatory Government built the steel construction to keep the building from crumbling; it remains to this day.

Then took they the body of Jesus, and wound it in linen clothes with the spices.

ANOINTING OF JESUS' BODY

And after this Joseph of Arimathaea, being a disciple of Jesus, but secretly for fear of the Jews, besought Pilate that he might take away the body of Jesus: and Pilate gave him leave. He came therefore, and took the body of Jesus.

And there came also Nicodemus, which at the first came to Jesus by night, and brought a mixture of Myrrh and aloes, about an hundred pound weight. Then took they the body of Jesus, and wound it in linen clothes with the spices, as the manner of the Jews is to bury. *John 19:38-40*

The Stone of Anointment inside the Church of the Holy Sepulchre. Since 1810 this stone has belonged to all of the denominations that are represented in this church. It is the stone upon which the corpse of Jesus was supposed to have been placed when it was anointed. The oil paintings on the wall describe this scene.

Left: The interior of the Holy Sepulchre. A marble plate covers the Rock of the Tomb that was identified in 326 A.D. by Constantine as the tomb of Christ. Among the 43 oil lamps that are hanging in the tomb, 13 belong to the Latin (Catholic) church, 13 to the Greek, 13 to the Armenian, and 4 to the Coptic.

The Burial. A bronze relief in the altar of the Latin Golgotha Chapel, done by Portigianis in 1588.

*He came therefore, and took
the body of Jesus.*

And now when the even was come, because it was the preparation, that is, the day before the sabbath, Joseph of Arimathaea, an honourable counsellor, which also waited for the kingdom of God, came, and went in boldly unto Pilate, and craved the body of Jesus. And Pilate marvelled if he were already dead: and calling unto him the centurion, he asked him whether he had been any while dead. And when he knew it of the centurion, he gave the body to Joseph.

Mark 15:42-45

The Anointment of Jesus. A ceramic tile in the Etchmiadzin Chapel in the St. James Armenian Patriarchate Church. It was brought from Qutahia (Armenia) in the 17th century.

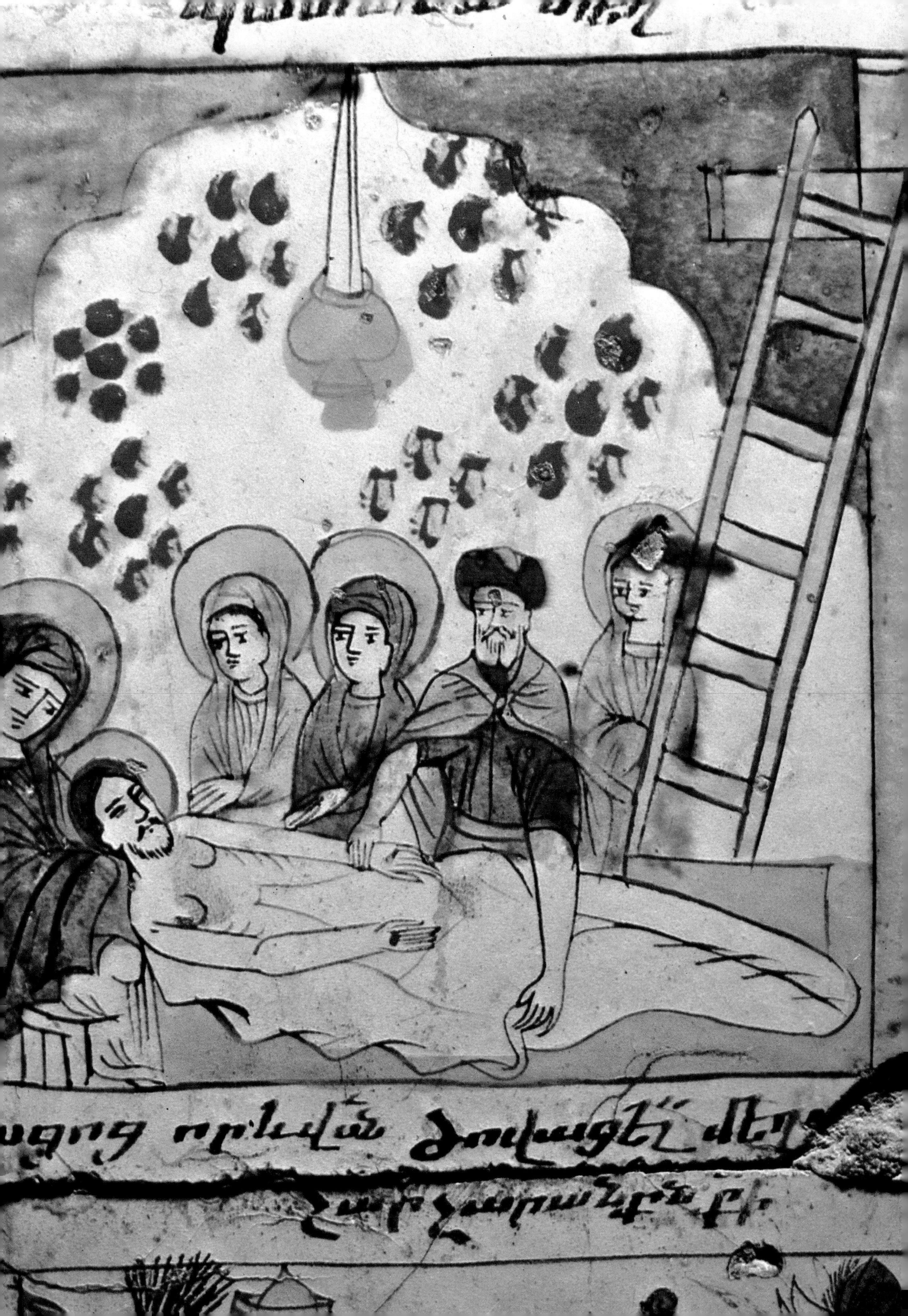

And in the garden a new sepulchre, wherein was never man yet laid.

The Garden Tomb discovered by General Gordon, who believed that he had found the original tomb of Jesus. Even though much archeological evidence shows that this tomb is of a Byzantine architecture, it is a good example of a typical private rock tomb.

THE TOMB OF JESUS

Now in the place where he was crucified there was a garden; and in the garden a new sepulchre wherein was never man yet laid. There laid they Jesus therefore because of the Jews' preparation day; for the sepulchre was nigh at hand.

John 19:41-42

And when Joseph had taken the body, he wrapped it in a clean linen cloth, and laid it in his own new tomb, which he had hewn out in the rock: and he rolled a great stone to the door of the sepulchre, and departed. *Matt. 27:59-60*

The tomb has an entrance room and a main burial chamber. In the chamber there is room for three, but two of the grave pits are unfinished.

A Jewish family grave which, according to tradition, belonged to Joseph of Arimathea. The entrance to the grave is through the Syrian Jacobite Chapel in the Rotunda of the Holy Sepulchre Church. This proves that this whole area was, in the time of Christ, outside the city wall, because the Jews did not bury their dead inside the city itself.

A view into the Chapel of St. Helena. This Byzantine construction lies underneath the Church of the Holy Sepulchre and is connected with that church through a stairway This chapel is dedicated to the Empress Helena and belongs to the Armenian church. The crosses in the stones can be found in all the ancient churches and date from the time of the Crusaders.

The Grotto in which the cross was found, with the Chapel of St. Helena in the background. According to tradition, the Empress Helena, mother of Emperor Constantine, found the cross of Jesus at this place which was previously a cistern. The small window at upper right is called "the chair of Helena." There she was supposed to have sat and directed the search for the cross. Every year on May 3rd the Festival of the Finding of the Cross is commemorated with a Pontifical celebration.

Why seek ye the living among the dead?

THE EMPTY TOMB

Now upon the first day of the week, very early in the morning, they came unto the sepulchre, bringing the spices which they had prepared, and certain others with them. And they found the stone rolled away from the sepulchre. And they entered in, and found not the body of the Lord Jesus. And it came to pass, as they were much perplexed thereabout, behold, two men stood by them in shining garments; And as they were afraid, and bowed down their faces to the earth, they said unto them, Why seek ye the living among the dead? He is not here, but is risen: remember how he spake unto you when he was yet in Galilee, saying, The Son of man must be delivered into the hands of sinful men, and be crucified, and the third day rise again. And they remembered his words, and returned from the sepulchre, and told all these things unto the eleven, and to all the rest. It was Mary Magdalene, and Joanna, and Mary the mother of James, and other women that were with them, which told these things unto the apostles. And their words seemed to them as idle tales, and they believed them not.

Luke 24:1-11

The Angel and the two Marys near the empty tomb. A ceramic tile from the Etchmiadzin Chapel in the St. James Armenian Patriarchate Church. The tile was brought from Qutahia (Armenia) in the seventeenth century.

The Holy of Holies in the small Ethiopian Chapel on the roof of the Holy Sepulchre.

Left: The Holy of Holies in the Ethiopian Church of Mea-Shearim.

The Resurrection of Christ. An icon in the Church of the Nativity in Bethlehem. Oil on wood.

The Resurrection of Christ, as the Greek inscription in the picture indicates. This oil on wood icon is in the Holy of Holies in the Church of the Nativity. It was given to the church in 1843.

St. Constantine and St. Helena with the cross of Christ. An icon from the Church of the Nativity in Bethlehem, oil on wood. The Greek inscription means "of the Holy King Constantine and Queen Helena."

Right: The Coptic Chapel at the back of the Holy Tomb, inside the Rotunda of the Church of the Holy Sepulchre. The Coptics show underneath the altar what is believed to be a piece of the original rock of the tomb. The chapel has belonged to the Coptic Church since 1573.

Whose soever sins ye remit, they are remitted unto them; and whose soever sins ye retain, they are retained.

THE RISEN LORD

And as they thus spake, Jesus himself stood in the midst of them, and saith unto them, Peace be unto you. But they were terrified and affrighted, and supposed that they had seen a spirit. And he said unto them, Why are ye troubled? and why do thoughts arise in your hearts? Behold my hands and my feet, that it is I myself: handle me, and see; for a spirit hath not flesh and bones, as ye see me have. And when he had thus spoken, he shewed them his hands and his feet. And while they yet believed not for joy, and wondered, he said unto them, Have ye here any meat? And they gave him a piece of a broiled fish, and of an honeycomb. And he took it, and did eat before them. *Luke 24:36-43*

Then the same day at evening, being the first day of the week, when the doors were shut where the disciples were assembled for fear of the Jews, came Jesus and stood in the midst, and saith unto them, Peace be unto you. And when he had so said, he shewed unto them his hands and his side. Then were the disciples glad, when they saw the Lord. Then said Jesus to them again, Peace be unto you: as my Father hath sent me, even so send I you. And when he had said this, he breathed on them, and saith unto them, Receive ye the Holy Ghost: Whose soever sins ye remit, they are remitted unto them; and whose soever sins ye retain, they are retained. *John 20:19-23*

Mass in front of the Holy Tomb.

Blessed are they that have not seen, and yet have believed.

DOUBTING THOMAS

But Thomas, one of the twelve, called Didymus, was not with them when Jesus came. The other disciples therefore said unto him, We have seen the Lord. But he said unto them, Except I shall see in his hands the print of the nails and put my finger into the print of the nails, and thrust my hand into his side, I will not believe.

And after eight days again his disciples were within, and Thomas with them: then came Jesus, the doors being shut, and stood in the midst, and said, Peace be unto you. Then saith he to Thomas, Reach hither thy finger, and behold my hands; and reach hither thy hand, and thrust it into my side: and be not faithless, but believing. And Thomas answer·ed and said unto him, My Lord and my God. Jesus saith unto him, Thomas, because thou hast seen me, thou hast believed: blessed are they that have not seen, and yet have believed. *John 20:24-29*

Doubting Thomas. A colored ceramic tile in the Etchmiadzin Chapel in the St. James Armenian Patriarchate Church.

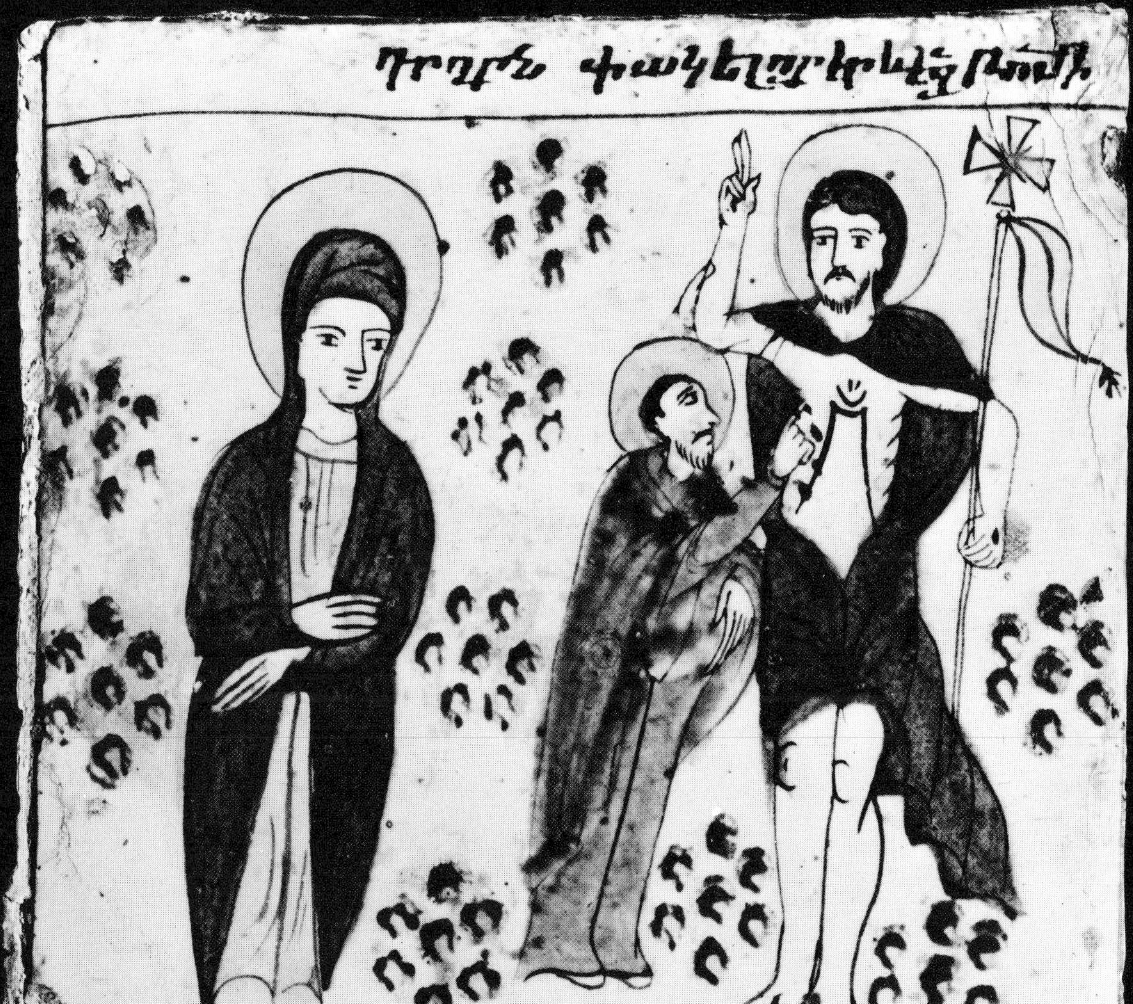

The Angel's Chapel at the entrance room to the Holy Tomb. The chapel is dedicated to the angel who spoke to the women on the morning of Easter Sunday. At the center is a piece of stone that was used to seal the opening of the tomb. This piece of stone is covered with marble plates and has a glass cover on the top. Some tourist guides tell the pilgrims that this was the stone upon which the angel once sat.

154

And many other signs truly did Jesus in the presence of his disciples, which are not written in this book: But these are written, that ye might believe that Jesus is the Christ, the Son of God; and that believing ye might have life through his name.   *John 20:30-31*

Jerusalem in Old Testament times

Medieval and Turkish Jerusalem

Approximate lines of City Walls:
of original Zion (2 Sam. 5. 7)
as extended under the kings
as extended later, either
before or after the Exile
Modern Roads

Heights are given in feet

0   500 Yards

0   500 Metres

TURKISH WALL

2,525

2,583

?Gate of Benjamin

?Hananel

Baris

2,490

NEW
CITY
(MISHNA,
SECOND QUARTER)

TEMPLE · 2,435
□ □ ALTAR

?PALACE

Valley

?Gennath Gate

(LOWER CITY) Wall

2,542

?MILLO

Solomon's

UPPER
CITY

Central (Cheesemakers)

Manasseh's Wall

2,525 ·

TURKISH WALL

Gate

Water
Shaft

·Gihon Spring

Wall of Zion

CITY OF DAVID

?Upper
Pool

Mount of Olives

OPHEL

Conduit

Old-Conduit

Post-exilic
Jewish tombs

Monument of
Beni Hezir

SILOAM

Kidron Valley

Hezekiah's

Hinnom

Lower Pool
between the walls

Old Pool

Gate

Pre-exilic Jewish cemetery

Gate

Gate

Valley (? T o p h e t h)

En-rogel
o Spring

Based on the Oxford Bible Atlas

© Oxford University Press